I0366895

Careers in Animal Care and Veterinary Science

Deborah A. Marinelli

The Rosen Publishing Group, Inc.
New York

Thanks to Annie L. Sommers and Erica MacKenzie Smith.

Published in 2001 by The Rosen Publishing Group, Inc.
29 East 21st Street, New York, NY 10010

Copyright © 2001 by Deborah A. Marinelli

First Edition

All rights reserved. No part of this book may be reproduced in any form without permission in writing from the publisher, except by a reviewer.

Cover photo © Wildlife Conservation Society, Headquarters at the Bronx Zoo

Library of Congress Cataloging-in-Publication Data

Marinelli, Deborah A.
   Careers in animal care and veterinary science / by Deborah A. Marinelli.
      p. cm. — (Careers)
   Includes bibliographical references (p.) and index.
   ISBN 978-1-4358-8638-4
   1. Animal specialists—Vocational guidance—United States—Juvenile literature. 2. Veterinary medicine—Vocational guidance—United States—Juvenile literature. [1. Animal specialists—Vocational guidance 2. Veterinary medicine—Vocational guidance 3. Vocational guidance.] I. Title. II. Careers (Rosen Publishing Group).
   SF80 .M358 2000
   636'.023'73—dc21   00-009720

Manufactured in the United States of America

About the Author

Deborah Aydt Marinelli holds a Ph.D. in English from the State University of New York at Albany and an M.A. in liberal education from St. John's College, Santa Fe. A professional writer, researcher, and editor for twenty years, she has published fiction and nonfiction with Scholastic Books Division, Playboy Press, John Knox Press, and Great Source/Houghton Mifflin Publishing Companies. She also teaches writing at Hudson Valley Community College in Troy, New York. Marinelli lives in Kinderhook, New York, with her husband, Lorenzo, and her eighteen-year-old terrier mix dog, Edna.

Contents

Introduction		1
1.	A Wide Range of Career Choices	2
2.	Animal Care Through the Ages	9
3.	Doctors of the Animal Kingdom	13
4.	Veterinarians Get to Choose What They Do	22
5.	Like a Nurse to a Doctor: The Veterinary Technician	29
6.	Training Animals to Work and Live with Humans	34
7.	Breeding Animals Is Big Business	51
8.	The Boarding Business: Simple Pet-Sitting to Luxury Pet Hotels	55
9.	Animal Makeovers: The Groomer's World	58
10.	Pet Store Owners and Marketers	62
11.	Zoologists Classify the Animal Kingdom	66
12.	Marine Biologists: Getting into the Swim	70
13.	Animal Adoption Workers Provide Love and Homes for Unwanted Pets	73
14.	Saving the Whales and Other Animals	78
15.	The Future of Animal Care	81
16.	Getting Started in an Animal Care Profession	87

Glossary	91
Appendix A: Animal Interest and Protection Groups	93
Appendix B: Veterinary Medical Associations	98
Appendix C: Recommended Web Sites and Journals	112
For Further Reading	116
Index	119

Introduction

If you enjoy a special bond with animals and like the work it takes to keep them well fed, groomed, and exercised, you may be a natural candidate for a career in animal care. Few jobs offer the instant rewards of seeing a sick and listless animal restored to health, a bedraggled pet spruced up and proud after a grooming session, or a four-legged beast transformed into a four-legged friend after your training instructions have taken hold. Nor are there many careers where your clients will respond with a purr, a wag, and unquestioning devotion.

There's no need to worry about the growth potential in this field. Today, Americans care for about 59 million cats, 53 million dogs, 13 million birds, 4 million horses, 6 million rabbits and ferrets, 5 million rodents, 3.5 million reptiles, and 56 million fish! That's according to a study conducted in 1996 by the American Veterinary Medical Association (AVMA). The majority of U.S. households—59 percent—own at least one pet.

Animal care practitioners usually love their work because they've found a way to create a productive professional life that's in sync with their natural interests. It's not uncommon for veterinarians and veterinary technicians to have spent their childhood years bandaging friends' cats and dogs and sneaking food to neighborhood strays. As adults, they've refined their early skills to become healers and rescuers for the animal kingdom.

1

A Wide Range of Career Choices

Few career fields offer such a broad range of choices as animal care. If you have exceptional academic abilities and top grades, you may want to consider becoming a veterinarian. Be aware, though, that in some states, it is harder to get into a college of veterinary medicine than it is to win admission to a traditional medical school. This is because there are fewer places available for candidates. To be competitive, you'll want to take a college prep program in high school that includes lots of science and math. Standardized test scores make a difference, too, so it may pay to take a commercial SAT or ACT preparation course to help you climb into the higher percentiles. Competition is tough, but the rewards—both monetary and psychological—will make your hard work worthwhile.

Your choices continue after veterinary college admission, for a doctor of veterinary medicine (DVM) has opportunities to focus on a variety of fascinating specialties, such as large animal, small animal, wildlife, equine (horse), holistic, exotic animal, and agribusiness practices. Most DVMs study for a minimum of four years following a minimum of ninety credits of undergraduate course work in a general college program. Internships and residencies,

A Wide Range of Career Choices

should a new doctor choose to pursue them, take additional years of work.

If the idea of so many years of study doesn't appeal to you, or if you want or need to earn income in the near future, you can make a place for yourself as an indispensable member of the veterinary health care team with just two years of specialized training.

The **veterinary technician**, as this team member is called, works closely with a supervising veterinarian, performing many of the same tasks that a nurse might perform for a doctor. Veterinary technicians assist with diagnostic, medical, and surgical procedures for which they have been specially trained, almost always in laboratory settings using live animals. Most of them are employed in private practice, but the demand for technicians in other areas such as diagnostic laboratories, zoos and wildlife facilities, biomedical facilities, the military, and humane societies is on the upswing. Veterinary technicians earn salaries that compare to those earned by workers with similar educational levels in other fields. Testing, certification, and registration requirements—the credentials that permit a veterinary technician to work legally—vary from state to state.

Animal trainers provide an important link between our species and the animal kingdom. Their work enables humans with special needs to live independently with service animals such as Seeing Eye, Hearing Ear, and seizure-sensitive dogs. Trainers also coach the courageous search and rescue dogs so often photographed in life-saving activities after an earthquake or bombing, or when hikers and campers become lost in the wild. Dogs also are trained by the police to track criminals and to sniff for evidence of incendiary devices or illegal drugs. In addition to service and rescue animals, talented trainers coach exotic animals who star as circus performers, as well as animals featured in the movies and on television. Trainers prepare for their careers in various ways. Some of these trainers are DVMs and veterinary technicians, but others have graduated from an association's training program or have amassed their knowledge over many years by taking a series of master classes and seminars. Typically, there are more applicants wanting to work in this field than there are jobs, so formal training and preparation can provide a critical edge when you seek entry-level employment. Salaries vary widely, with each employer setting his or her own standards. The animal training field also has a high percentage of self-employed workers.

Animal breeders work to replenish the supply of pets, livestock, and exotic wildlife. The education you'll need to work in this field varies from DVM or Ph.D. certification to informal on-your-own study, if you want to breed cats or dogs. It's almost simplistic to talk about an animal breeder as if this was one job category, because the work varies so tremendously depending on the animal you're talking about. Your job may be exotic and a big-budget enterprise, such as supervising the nearly two-year-long pregnancy of an elephant or encouraging rare pandas to breed in captivity. The breeding of alpacas, cousins to llamas, has become popular in the United States recently because a yearly return of 58 percent can be realized on a start-up investment. There are about 700 alpaca breeders in the country who sell the animals' particularly soft fur to home weavers for $3 to $5 per ounce. This means that

A Wide Range of Career Choices

a newborn alpaca is worth about $18,000! Is it any wonder that animal breeding is of interest to bright and ambitious young people?

Dogs and cats, the focus of the most common breeding operations, are mated to assure breed purity; but there can be problems, especially among puppy breeders. In California, a state-funded investigation revealed that about 25 percent of purebred dogs on the market have some genetic disease. For example, one breed's drooping eyes are a prized feature, but this has been enhanced by a thyroid problem. A new state bill would fine breeders up to $10,000 if they knowingly sell defective pups and ban the breeders from the business for up to ten years. States are also watching dog and cat breeders closely to encourage them to become more like larger businesses, paying sales taxes when they market puppies or kittens. Some states are looking at breeding laws that will require pet breeders to buy a $100 license, the registration number of which will have to be published whenever an advertisement is run. As you can see, pet breeding is becoming more like a big retail business—not surprising when you learn that big states like California produce approximately half a million purebred puppies each year.

Livestock such as cattle, lambs, sheep, swine, and poultry are bred for maximum food or animal-product yield. The work of a breeder may take place in a sophisticated scientific laboratory, utilizing cutting-edge fertilization or cloning technology, or the animals may reproduce naturally in a rural setting. The income potential in this field ranges from the high incomes of commercial breeders to the moderate part-time incomes generally earned by workers in "cottage industry" operations or on family farms. Thoroughbred horse breeders work in a world of their own, in which champion racers can generate hundreds of thousands of dollars in stud fees.

With an increasingly prosperous workforce and retiree set engaged in frequent business and personal travel, **animal boarders and groomers** are experiencing a boom in business. Animal boarding is usually offered by veterinary clinics, so veterinarians and veterinary technicians frequently act as overnight hosts for their clients' pets. In recent years, some of these clinics have begun to offer optional grooming services as well as animal caretaking. Independent pet groomers also offer skin, coat, and nail care to clients, as well as spa treatments and flea and parasite control. There are also exciting opportunities to groom racing and entertainment animals, including those who appear as regular performers on series TV shows. You can complete groomer's school in a matter of weeks, and the cost of your tuition usually includes a professional start-up kit. Licensure and certification requirements for boarders and groomers vary from state to state, but some states are moving in the direction of requiring governmental oversight, as well as quality standards established by trade associations. Fees and salaries in these fields vary widely according to each provider's credentials and location—but with more Americans buying and adopting pets each year, these are definitely career fields with a future.

Opportunities for **pet store owners and marketers** have undergone tremendous changes in recent years, as marketing conglomerates have pioneered the establishment of pet superstores, providing everything from puppy kibble to exotic reptiles and amphibians.

A Wide Range of Career Choices

Some of these stores even work with veterinarians and technicians to offer vaccination services and grooming services on-site. Others offer basic and advanced obedience training for a fee. However, mall and neighborhood pet stores still dominate in midsize communities. Entry-level training opportunities in pet and pet product marketing may pay the minimum wage for caring for the animals on sale and restocking food and products, but the owner of a pet megastore can make millions. The rules of this market are being further rewritten by Internet sales. As this book goes to press, a handful of e-commerce pet stores have gone on-line, one with the announced goal of "becoming the Amazon.com of pet product marketing." Though in many states, pet stores are subject to governmental review of sanitary conditions, the Internet businesses promise to become very entrepreneurial. These are less regulated and are wide open to creative thinkers with business credentials, as well as animal care backgrounds.

Animal conservationists (also called **preservationists**) have a major effect on global ecosystems, as they engage in the fight to save rare animals and endangered species from extinction. They range from Ph.D.s with extensive laboratory and field experience to committed volunteers. **Zoologists** may have bachelor's degrees in zoology, but often they also have a DVM and/or a Ph.D. in a specialized research field. **Marine biologists** range from those with a bachelor's degree to those with a Ph.D. They may work in aquariums or for public or private foundations engaged in oceanic research. **Animal control workers** have varied credentials. They may be veterinary technicians, or they may qualify for their positions by taking civil service tests and demonstrating that they have experience in animal care. Although animal control workers must be prepared to supervise humane euthanasia of abandoned animals, these workers also develop community support for neutering and adoption programs.

In the upcoming chapters, we will look more closely at these animal care careers and the preparation it takes to pursue each one.

Animal Care Through the Ages

The earliest pet was probably a dog, but we are unsure exactly how the human-pet bond first developed. Scientists think that the special relationship between human beings and canines probably began when wild wolves experienced an evolutionary leap. It's a mystery whether a new, tamer breed of wolf attached itself to humans, or whether humans were first to think of animals as companions. Experts point out, though, that the question of intention—whether a species, human or wolf, *meant* to befriend the other—is beside the point. Domestication of animals was not just one isolated event, but rather a long and complex process.[1] And however it developed, the human-pet bond grew beyond the sharing of food to include the sharing of affection and companionship. This is why, in most veterinary colleges, pets are called companion animals.

As early as 9000 BC, Middle Eastern herders used crude medical skills to keep their sheep healthy. These skills became more sophisticated in the hands of Egyptians from about 4000 to 300 BC. Papyrus fragments from an Egyptian medical textbook dated around 1850 BC describe diseases of cattle, dogs, birds, and fish. These records reveal that Egyptians understood animal anatomy and knew how to make sick animals better. Evidence of animal medicine has also been found in the

---

[1]Trut, Lyudmila N., *American Scientist,* v. 87, Mar./Apr. 1999, p. 160.

ancient Babylonian, Hindu, Hebrew, Arab, Greek, and Roman civilizations.

Moreover, there is direct evidence that dogs were used as sophisticated service animals in ancient times. On the wall of a house in Pompeii that was buried in ash in the year AD 79, a painting depicts a woman and her maid in the marketplace being approached by what seems to be a blind man with a staff. He is apparently being led by a small dog, which in the painting is turning to his master as if seeking instructions.[2] The relationship depicted is almost identical to that between a modern-day Seeing Eye dog and his blind owner.

Pet grooming was documented in an Elizabethan-era lithograph of a dog being sheared while sitting in a lady's lap. In France during the time of King Louis XV, the poodle was the official dog of the court. The first records of dog-grooming parlors were kept during this time as well. *Ashmont's Kennel Secrets*, published in 1893 in Boston, gives some of the earliest printed grooming recommendations for standard breeds such as washing and coat conditioning.[3]

The first formal veterinary school was in France. It was founded in Lyons in 1761 and later became known as the Royal Veterinary School. Horses, cattle, and sheep illnesses were studied there. In America, the first veterinary institution was the Veterinary College of Philadelphia, which operated from 1852 until 1866. The School of Veterinary Medicine at the University of

---

[2] "Coon, Nelson, "Brief History of Dog Guides," 1929, published on Seeingeye.org

[3] Ogle, Madeline Bright, "From Problems to Profits," 1989 and 1997, published on www.petgroomer.com.

Pennsylvania, established in 1884, is the oldest accredited veterinary school still operating.[4] Founded on the recommendation of the university's school of medicine, this school had strong roots in human medical science.[5]

In 1822, animal lovers and caregivers were encouraged when the British Parliament passed a bill "to prevent cruel and improper treatment of cattle." In 1824, the Royal Society for the Prevention of Cruelty to Animals (RSPCA) was chartered. It took another forty-six years for America to follow suit, with the establishment of the American Society for the Prevention of Cruelty to Animals (ASPCA). The ASPCA's founder, Peter Bergh, was inspired to action when he saw peasants in Russia cruelly beating a horse. On his way home to America, he visited the RSPCA in London to learn how he could go about organizing against cruelty to animals. In the early days, the ASPCA usually dealt with the abuse of work animals, as pet owning in those days was relatively rare.

The adoption of pets did not became widespread in average families until the Victorian era, but chiefs of state and notables have always had pets.[6] Murals of Egyptian pharaohs show them in the company of sleek, greyhound-like dogs. George Washington owned thirty-six dogs, and Franklin D. Roosevelt's Scottish terrier, Fala, was almost as famous as the president who owned him. Jimmy Carter's dog, Grits, made page one news when he refused to let a veterinarian test him during Heartworm Awareness Week.

[4]www.encarta.msn.com.

[5]University of Pennsylvania School of Veterinary Medicine Communications Office.

[6]Motavalli, Jim, *E: The Environmental Magazine*, Sept./Oct. 1995, p. 38.

The popularizing of pet owning transformed old-fashioned "horse doctors" into real professionals who cared for all kinds of small pets as well as larger ranch, farm, sporting, and food animals. In these early days of formal veterinary practice, vets often competed with county agents, who also dispensed care to sick animals. The U.S. Department of Agriculture encouraged this practice because veterinarians were few in number. Misunderstandings between the two groups eventually were worked out. In some states, there were strong links between early veterinarians and the military. Texas, for example, which established its veterinary college at Texas A&M University, concentrated all services on guard dog training and care within the military.

Veterinary medicine has made enormous strides from the 1960s onward. The gender barrier was finally breached when women entered the profession in greater numbers. In 1997, the Association of Women Veterinarians celebrated its fiftieth anniversary, and in 1996 Dr. Mary Beth Leininger became the first woman president of the American Veterinary Medical Association. Only about 9 percent of veterinarians were female in 1980; today nearly a third of the 59,000 veterinarians who practice in the United States are women.[7] Diagnostic and preventative medicine became routine for both companion and food animals to the point where, except in the wild, the James Herriot–type of highly personal animal doctoring has virtually disappeared.[8] Today, modern veterinary science is on a par with human medicine, emphasizing technology, revolutionary drug therapies, state-of-the-art surgery, and all-species protection and care.

[7] www.vin.com/scripts/asp/features.asp.
[8] Friedberger, Mark, *Southwestern Historical Quarterly*, July 1993.

3

Doctors of the Animal Kingdom

More than 55,000 veterinarians currently practice in the United States, primarily in private hospitals and clinics—and over 2,000 new veterinarians begin their careers each year. Of these, more than half treat only small animals such as cats and dogs; 10 percent treat large animals such as cattle and other livestock; and about 4 percent treat horses. The remainder treat both large and small animals.[9]

WHAT MUST I DO TO BECOME A VETERINARIAN?

What does it take to become a veterinarian? Along with the ability to meet the rigorous admission requirements to the veterinary college of your choice, you will need some specific personal qualities. You should enjoy a special rapport with animals. It helps to be gentle and calm, as many of your patients will be skittish during examinations. Pet owners consider their animals to be extensions of the family circle, and they expect veterinarians to provide the same quality of care as a human doctor would. You should be detail oriented because record keeping can make a life-or-death difference in any animal hospital. Because a sick spaniel can easily mistake your waiting room for a favorite tree, having an easygoing temperament and a sense of humor is a great advantage. In addition, you

[9]www.encarta.msn.com.

should be dedicated to the concept of preventative care: Performing well-animal checkups and preventative services such as vaccinations and puppy worming will avoid many expensive and complex problems down the line.

Did you know that a simple vaccination for cats keeps deadly feline leukemia at bay, or that an early treatment against heartworm can save the life of a dog? Or did you know that the application of routine flea and tick repellent can keep an animal from contracting debilitating Lyme disease? Should you become a veterinarian, one of your most important responsibilities will be to educate pet owners about the tremendous benefits of early care and prevention.

These days, you need to be very smart and competitive to get into a veterinary college. As mentioned earlier, there are more colleges for the practice of human medicine than for animal medical care. As a result, the admissions process for veterinary students is very complex. To win a place, you'll need to take the Veterinary Aptitude Test (VAT), Medical College Admission Test (MCAT), and/or the Graduate Record Examination (GRE). You'll need to score well on these standardized tests because most veterinary colleges "go by the numbers" when they choose students. You'll also need positive letters of reference from teachers, sponsors, and anyone who has supervised your work with animals.

Most veterinary colleges assign a weight of about 20 percent to a student's work experience with animals, so, for example, working part-time or volunteering in an ASPCA shelter can mean the difference between success and failure when you apply. It may also strengthen your application to get experience with a variety of species, not just cats and dogs. The quality of your experience is considered, too: a young man or woman who trained search and rescue dogs for the military would be viewed very favorably, as would someone who cared for animals in controlled conditions in a scientific laboratory. These are examples of work experiences that would carry more weight than, say, dog walking for your neighbors, though any animal care experience should be included on your application.

Sometimes would-be veterinarians are fortunate enough to learn of mentoring programs that are tailor-made to help them along. In North Carolina, the Cooperative Extension Service sponsors the Veterinary Explorer Program in which about twenty high school students meet monthly for an in-depth, hands-on look at careers in veterinary medicine. Participants collaborate with local veterinarians and health department workers to coordinate and promote a rabies vaccination clinic and a prepaid spay-neuter program at the local animal shelter. These are the sorts of tasks that any veterinary college would view favorably. In addition, these students conduct joint research on employment patterns, job outlook, and the projected earnings of future veterinarians. Try calling the Cooperative Extension Service of your home county to see if the agents know of any similar program close to your home.

Committees often search for evidence of your character, documented either by a record of your community service or by other proof that you are responsible and giving. Your leadership qualities will also be reviewed. Of course, a solid record of academic achievement is the single most important requirement. High school students who want to be veterinarians are encouraged to take biology, chemistry, physics, calculus, trigonometry, statistics, environmental/earth science, and English. This sounds like, and is, quite an assortment of subjects, but veterinarians have to do more than just care for animals. They must communicate effectively with human owners, compute correct dosages of drugs, be knowledgeable about city licensing requirements, maintain detailed records, and even deal with the Internal Revenue Service each April 15. Rest assured, none of the knowledge you acquire in high school and college will be wasted.

Before you can be admitted to veterinary college, you'll almost always need to finish four years of undergraduate college education. (Some veterinary colleges permit high-performing sophomores to apply for admission following their junior year in college.) Any major is acceptable, as long as it requires you to include plenty of math and science in your program of study. You'll want to attend the most selective undergraduate college you possibly can because most veterinary colleges assign "points" to undergraduate programs. Some admissions committees measure the college you have attended by using the *Peterson's Guide to Four Year Colleges* ranking system. It doesn't matter if you attended a public or private college, or how much you paid in tuition. What admissions committees are interested in is how high the academic standards you had to meet were and how good your grades were compared to those of other students.

The following grid outlines an academic program that would make a favorable impression on a typical veterinary college's admissions committee. Notice the number of courses in hard science.

Pre-Vet Course Work[10]

1st Year	English composition	Biology or Zoology	General chemistry
2nd Year	Organic chemistry	General physics	Calculus (recommended)
3rd Year	Biochemistry (half-year)	Microbiology (half-year)	GRE preparation seminar (recommended)

WHAT HAPPENS ONCE I'M ACCEPTED AS A STUDENT?

When you receive the letter stating that you have been accepted by a veterinary college, your hard work is just beginning. Once you arrive, you'll undertake a program of study that offers you both regular and laboratory/clinical classroom learning experiences. You'll sit in on lectures, conduct library research, make your way through interactive computer programs, and participate with small groups in clinical exercises. You'll also probably be able to take care of at least some of your requirements via the Internet, which will offer you the comfort and convenience of working from home.

Not only will you be learning how to provide medical care to animals, you'll be perfecting communications skills, ethics, professional development, and clinical practices. You'll learn about zoonotic diseases (animal diseases that can be transmitted to humans) and the role veterinary medicine plays in the overall spectrum of public health. There are also important

---
[10] Provided by the Cornell College of Veterinary Medicine.

public service roles veterinarians undertake. For example, the American Veterinary Medical Association currently is using its clout to lobby Congress to permit residents in public housing to own pets. As laws are currently written, responsible families who have a well-cared-for, well-behaved cat or dog are in danger of being evicted. Massachusetts, which has a successful "responsible pet owners" program for families on public assistance, is leading the way in this educational crusade. This state features tenant "pet committees" that require the payment of a pet deposit and spaying or neutering, plus establishing clear expectations for both tenants and landlords. Wherever you decide to live, it's not at all unusual for veterinarians to be drafted onto citizen action committees, particularly study groups that have an impact on wildlife or public health concerns.

Another thing you can look forward to as a veterinary student is the chance to make clinical rotations in each animal care specialty. This will help you determine if you have an interest in any particular specialty area. You were attracted to veterinary science in the first place by your love of working with animals, and the closer you get to graduation, the more time you'll be permitted to spend working with them. As your program of study progresses, you'll move from observing treatments, to assisting during treatments, and finally to performing them independently under the watchful eyes of graduate veterinarians. The following chart outlines a typical four-year program in veterinary medicine.[11] Notice the clinical rotations students are assigned to make during their junior and

[11]Curriculum of Cornell College of Veterinary Medicine.

senior years. By the time all of your classes and requirements are completed, you will have studied and worked for over 4,000 hours.

	Fall Semester	**Spring Semester**
1st Year	The Animal Body Genetics & Development	Distribution courses Function & Dysfunction/ Part 1
2nd Year	Function & Host, Agent & Defense Function & Dysfunction/ Part 2	Distribution courses Animal Health & Disease/ Part 1
3rd Year	Animal Health & Disease/ Part 2	Distribution courses Clinical rotations
4th Year	Clinical rotations	Distribution courses Clinical rotations

As you see, you will get to take a number of distribution courses—this is what electives are called in most veterinary colleges. Other courses, such as "The Animal Body," fall into the foundation course category—in other words, these are courses students are required to take. These compulsory subjects make up about 70 percent of a student's total course load.

INTERNSHIPS, RESIDENCIES, AND BOARD CERTIFICATION

Veterinary graduates can go to work immediately following graduation. An internship is not required. Rather, it is an optional postgraduate program that provides training for setting up a practice, clinical teaching, and board-specialty knowledge. (A board is a panel of experts empowered to certify you in your specialty.) Interns and residents receive a salary during their work/training programs and participate as junior members of the medical team. As they gain experience, they are introduced to such areas as anesthesia, fluid therapy, intensive care, internal medicine, oncology, and radiology. They carry out tests, administer treatments, and monitor patients. They also have the opportunity to help specialists deliver advanced veterinary treatments such as cataract surgery, chemotherapy, radiation therapy, orthopedic surgery, dental treatments, and blood transfusions.[12] Only when you complete an internship, residency, and qualifying tests or reviews, can you call yourself a board-certified veterinarian.

In deciding which internship and residency applicants to accept, quite a few veterinary colleges use the services of the American Association of Veterinary Clinicians (AAVC) Intern/Resident Matching Program. In this program, internship and residency applicants rank veterinary schools in their order of preference. Veterinary schools do the same thing, only ranking the candidates in order of their qualifications. The matching process is automatic, so there is no guarantee that either applicants or schools will receive their top choices. The benefit of this service is that it is almost 100 percent fair and objective.

As a resident, you will gain experience that helps you to meet all the requirements of your specialty's board approval process. Residencies can take different amounts of time to complete. The following chart will help you to get a general idea of how long it will take to earn board certification in your chosen area.

[12]University of Pennsylvania.

How Long Will My Veterinary Residency Take?[13]

Ambulatory Medicine	Minimum of 2 Years
Anesthesiology	Minimum of 2 Years
Behavior	Minimum of 2 Years
Cardiology	Minimum of 2 Years
Dermatology	Minimum of 2 Years
Diagnostic Imaging	Minimum of 4 Years
Large Animal Medicine	Minimum of 2 Years
Small Animal Medicine	Minimum of 2 Years
Ophthalmology	Minimum of 3 Years
Large Animal Surgery	Minimum of 3 Years
Small Animal Surgery	Minimum of 3 Years

[13] Courtesy Cornell Veterinary Teaching Hospital.

4

Veterinarians Get to Choose What They Do

As you've already seen, it is possible for veterinarians to choose from among several different animal care specialties. Sometimes these specialties are circumscribed by the size of animal (large or small), its type (exotic, wild) or by the specific body part requiring treatment (ophthalmology, dermatology). The employer you work for may influence the kind of specialty you move into. (Or, conversely, you may choose an employer in order to practice your academic specialty.) For example, Dr. Dave Jessup, who works for the California Department of Fish and Wildlife, has become one of the leading experts in the world on the safe and gentle capture of wild animals. Jessup and his experiences are the subject of a new National Wildlife Federation documentary, *Wildlife Vet*, which airs on TBS. One of the first segments will examine trunk paralysis, a mysterious malady that is killing elephants in Matusadona National Park in Zimbabwe.[14]

Veterinarian Lucy Spelman treats geriatric—that is, very old—patients at the National Zoological Park in Washington, DC. Sea lions Maureen and Esther are both twenty-two years old—ancient, when you consider that few make it past fifteen. Esther takes steroids for muscle soreness and Maureen has a chronic infection

---

[14]Holmes, Bob, "Adventuring in the Field with One of the World's Leading Wildlife Vets," *National Wildlife*, Aug./Sept. 1998.

resulting from a bite, requiring antibiotics that cost more than $1,000 per month. In addition, Dr. Spelman treats a forty-seven-year-old hippo, a forty-one-year-old crocodile, and a thirty-five-year-old flamingo. Her days among these animal senior citizens are not unlike the days a human physician specializing in geriatric care would spend, though communications with old animals typically are more challenging.

Though it is uncommon, every once in a while you see a case where a human doctor crosses over into animal care. Dr. Sara de Sanz of San Francisco, a doctor of dental science for humans, provides an interesting example; she has developed a lively practice moonlighting as a dentist for exotic animals like baboons, elephants, and Bengal tigers.

Finally, Ph.D. specialists—who also are called doctors, though they conduct research and write dissertations instead of doing clinical rounds and internships—may work in such areas as immunology, toxicology, and physiology. These research doctors join animal care teams when their special expertise is needed. One example of when this might happen is when diseases that threaten human and animal health, such as tuberculosis, undulant fever, and rabies, threaten a population.

An overview of some of the most popular veterinary specialties follows.

BASIC ANIMAL PRACTICE SPECIALTIES

Small Animal   As it sounds, this area of animal medicine is devoted to small (usually companion) animals; heavy emphasis is on vaccination, treatment of illness and injury, parasite screens, neutering, husbandry, and humane euthanasia.

Large Animal	Practice for the larger patient, who ages at a faster rate and experiences specific body-type maladies; livestock are a central focus; services include vaccination, parasite control, neutering, and husbandry; equine practice is about 10 percent.
Exotic Animal	Animal medicine focused on unusual pets and wildlife such as snakes, frogs, and zoo animals; common services include obstetrics, surgery, habitat analysis, and preventative therapies.
Geriatric Practice	Focuses on caring for the older animal's specific problems, such as cognitive dysfunction, calcium degeneration, nutrition, and preventative therapies.
Ophthalmology	Specializes in animal vision therapies, including state of the art corneal laser procedures.
Cardiology	Treats heart problems of animals, including heart bypass surgeries.
Behavior	Specializes in animal behaviors such as aggression, depression, or dementia.
Anesthesiology	Sedates so that invasive treatments and therapies can be administered without pain to the animal.
Radiology	Performs diagnostic imaging of animals such as X rays, CAT scans, and MRIs.

Holistic Practices

A large number of animal caregivers, both doctors of veterinary medicine and other kinds of healers, specialize in a kind of health care called holistic. According to the American Holistic Veterinary Society, the techniques used in holistic medicine are gentle, minimally invasive, and emphasize patient well-being and stress reduction. These clinicians like to focus on genetics, nutrition, the environment, and the relationship between the pet and its owner, as well as herbal and natural medicines. Until the late 1990s, veterinarians

Veterinarians Get to Choose What They Do

did not express much interest in holistic care, but in 1996 the AVMA published an official set of guidelines on what it called "complementary" therapies.

Dr. David Jagger, former executive director of the International Veterinary Acupuncture Society, explained, "There is not a controlled study for everything. We use science whenever we can, but as practitioners we...also have to resort to artful applications."[15]

Alternate animal therapies currently in widespread use include acupuncture for conjunctivitis (a hard-to-treat eye disease), herbs for hairballs in cats, and dandelion for behavioral problems in horses and smaller mammals. Other common disorders that respond to such therapies include allergies, arthritis, parasites, and skin and coat problems.

Homeopathy is an old branch of medicine that has regained some favor in human treatment and is used to treat animals effectively as well. The motto of homeopathy is "like cures like." Samuel Christian Hahnemann, a nineteenth-century German medical doctor, developed this kind of medicine.

When a large dose of a toxic substance is swallowed, it can produce death. But when a homeopathic (greatly diluted) dose of the substance is given, it can save a poisoned animal. Homeopathic substances are derived from plants, minerals, drugs, viruses, bacteria, or animal substances and are said to contain "energy essences" that match the pattern present in a diseased animal.

Herbal therapies have been used to restore health and balance to the body in both human and animal medicine for centuries. Veterinary herbal medicines in

---

[15]Gorman, Christine, "Alternative Medicine for Dogs, Cats, and Cockatoos?" *Time*, Nov. 3, 1997.

current use include North American herbs, aryuvedic herbs from India, and Chinese traditional medicines.[16]

The most important sign that veterinary medicine is taking a serious interest in holistic treatment options is that a large number of veterinary colleges now offer distribution courses (electives) in these therapies. Angell Memorial Animal Hospital, Tufts School of Veterinary Medicine, and New York City's Animal Medical Center all practice acupuncture to varying degrees. The American Holistic Veterinary Medical Association, which was founded in 1982 by Dr. Carvel G. Tiekert and a small group of veterinarians, now includes over 300 animal healers who practice many different kinds of alternative therapies.[17] In 1996, Dr. Jan A. Bergeron and Dr. Susan Gayle Wynn took this healing philosophy to the public, when they created the AltVetMed Web site[18] with articles, frequently asked questions, and extensive links to similar pages.

Holistic medicine for animals is still more likely to be used in difficult cases than as frontline care, but the increasing number of "natural animal" publications, Web pages, and holistic veterinary products demonstrates the growing commitment to this type of animal care.

Agribusiness

Agriculture, and the role the veterinarian plays within it, has changed greatly over the last twenty years. Small family-owned farms are giving way to large corporate operations, and veterinarians are playing a key role in

---

[16] American Holistic Veterinary Association.
[17] Croke, Vicki, *Boston Globe,* Oct. 1, 1994.
[18] www.altvetmed.com.

Veterinarians Get to Choose What They Do

the safe production of both terrestrial (earth) and aquatic (water) food animals. Some veterinarians work in laboratories to perform diagnostic and testing reviews to screen for *E. coli* and other bacteria; others inspect animals and animal products and enforce quarantines when necessary; still others are specialists in the breeding and cloning of animals. Beef cattle, dairy, veal, swine, sheep, poultry, and fish are all inspected and treated by veterinarians, who must keep abreast of government regulations, international trade, and even financing practices within the food production industry. Most vets working in agribusiness are likelier to treat herds and groups than individual animals. Veterinarians working as food inspectors identify diseased livestock and unsafe meat and poultry. A primary part of their job is making sure that disease does not spread from animal to animal (or animal to human), and farm to farm.

Veterinary Salaries and Opportunities

If you want to be a veterinarian certified to do surgery on small animals, think about the amount of work it takes: four years of undergraduate college, another four years of veterinary training, then perhaps an additional four years of internship and residency. That adds up to a dozen years, or as much education as you've had in all your years of elementary and secondary school combined. No wonder young veterinarians, after their lengthy preparation, are interested in how much money they can earn!

The size of your salary will depend on where you choose to live and what kind of medicine you want to practice. AOL.com's Career Finder reports that the average veterinarian's salary was just over $55,000 in the year 2000. New graduates of the Mississippi State Veterinary College earn about $40,000—worth roughly the same since the cost of living in Mississippi is extremely low. The American Veterinary Association states that the actual starting salary for veterinarians in 1998 (the last year tallied) was $34,145 for men and $33,079 for women. Differences are due to the locations and kinds of practices of those interviewed and years in which the data were analyzed. On the high side, a dean/professor working for a veterinary college can earn almost $200,000 per year, and specialists who work in big city high-volume animal hospitals routinely break the $100,000 ceiling. For veterinarians who go into business for themselves, opening a chain of clinics or offering services and products over the Internet, the sky is the limit for earnings potential.

Several veterinary organizations report that, in recent years, salary growth has lagged behind that of comparable careers. One possible explanation for this is that the increasing number of women veterinarians has slowed salary increases. This is not because women don't earn the same actual salaries as men, but rather because they choose part-time schedules more often than men do. If money is your interest, a high-income state and high-volume practice will guarantee a very good living. If it's flexibility you're after, it has never been easier to work part-time and still earn enough income to support yourself and a family. More so than most other professionals, veterinarians control what they will earn and get to create whatever working conditions suit them.

5

Like a Nurse to a Doctor: The Veterinary Technician

If you like the company of animals, enjoy using your hands as well as your mind, and want to go to work in the near future instead of investing many years of your life in college study, a career in veterinary technology could be of interest to you.[19] Veterinary technicians are employed in a variety of clinical and laboratory settings.

A large variety of private practice opportunities exist in companion animal, food animal, equine, exotic animal, and mixed practices in every state. In animal clinics, the role of this trained professional is indispensable to the overall success of the veterinary team. Quite often, a veterinary technician is hired to manage an entire practice.

Other job opportunities include work in laboratories, biomedical facilities, zoos and wildlife facilities, the military, drug or feed manufacturing companies, food safety inspection sites, and colleges and universities.

Veterinary technicians perform many of the same services for a veterinarian that nurses perform for a medical doctor. They are usually the first to welcome a sick patient to the animal care clinic. The "vet tech" will assist in patient care, including pre- and postoperative procedures, and even sometimes perform dental prophylaxis

---

[19]Most veterinary technician information is provided by the AVMA's caretech Web site, www.avma.org./care4pets/caretech.

on animals. The American Veterinary Medical Association's "recommended skills and tasks" list for veterinary technologists includes such tasks as:

- Admit and discharge patients, take histories, maintain records, prepare appropriate certificates for signature
- Recognize different types and groups of drugs and calculate dosages; label and package dispensed drugs correctly
- Store, handle, and dispose of biologics and therapeutic agents, pesticides, and hazardous wastes
- Listen to heart and lungs using a stethoscope
- Assist with routine surgical and obstetrical procedures
- Maintain proper operating room conduct and sterile procedures
- Monitor anesthetic recovery and provide essential postoperative care; remove sutures
- Sterilize instruments and supplies using appropriate methods
- Induce and maintain general anesthesia
- Use a defibrillator
- Use crisis intervention/grief management skills with clients
- Operate/maintain suction and cautery machines

All veterinary technicians work under the guidance of doctors. They do not diagnose patients, perform surgery, or prescribe medicine without the supervision of a graduate DVM.

Educational Requirements

Educational requirements for this career usually begin with a two-year college degree. Some programs are longer in length and lead to a bachelor's or four-year degree, but these are much less common than the two-year model. There are over seventy-five AVMA-accredited programs in the United States. All of the best programs require that students work with live animals in a laboratory setting. (Some states are beginning to permit students to do some of their course work via distance learning, but this type of education is supplementary; it does not take the place of hands-on laboratory learning.) After gaining practical clinical experience, candidates for graduation (or in some states, new graduates) take standardized tests to prove that they are knowledgeable enough to work in the field.

There are different models of veterinary technology education, so you will want to review potential schools and colleges very carefully to make sure that you are in sync with their approach. Most colleges, for example, ask students to begin by taking regular liberal arts or "foundation" courses in the first year. In these programs, clinical experience comes as the last step of the academic cycle.

Some specialized schools focus on animal caregiving from the first day and do not require students to take classes in the liberal arts at all. A good test of a veterinary technology program is to check its Web page or call its career placement office to see how many veterinarians, laboratories, and clinics have listed job openings with a school. If there is a long list of postings for that college's or school's graduates, it's a good indication that the program is well regarded. Also check to see which associations the program belongs to. Don't hesitate to ask veterinarians how they feel about a local program. Chances are good that they've worked with its graduates and have an informed opinion.

National Sample of Veterinary Technician Salaries

Expertise	Range	Average Salary
Companion Animal Practice	$ 9,360 – 29,120	$17,226
Food Animal Practice	$ 9,360 – 24,900	$14,751
Equine Practice	$12,000 – 25,000	$15,293
Mixed Animal Practice	$10,000 – 36,800	$15,505
Specialty Practice	$10,000 – 34,000	$20,638
Industry/Sales	$12,000 – 70,000	$26,751
Veterinary Technician Education	$13,440 – 45,996	$24,614
Federal/State/Local Government	$ 9,420 – 36,000	$19,579
Diagnostics/ Research Lab	$ 9,420 – 43,680	$23,262
Other	Average Salary $23,262	Overall Average Salary $20,096

Source: 1994 Survey of Graduates (Most Recent)
Published by Department of Veterinary and Microbiological Sciences
North Dakota State University 8/21/96

Veterinary Technicians' Salaries and Benefits

Salaries and benefits compare favorably to those in other fields requiring a two-year college education. Just as with veterinarians, technicians' salaries are influenced by geographic location, years of experience, and the level of responsibility they have achieved. In March 2000, a scan of "Veterinary Technologist Wanted" advertisements across the country showed that an average salary range for new graduates is $8–$11 per hour, but almost all of these jobs also offered paid vacations, 401(k) plans, and health insurance, so the total package value was much greater than the listed hourly rate. In New York City, Weill Medical College of Cornell University posted a veterinary technologist position at a $38,720 minimum. In Fremont, California, Protein Design Labs wanted to hire a graduate for $2,083–$3,250 per month. Most position postings on the Internet state "Salaries DOE," which means that what you earn depends on the experience you bring to a given job. Once you have your associate's degree and certificate in hand, you will be in a good position to negotiate for an annual income you'll be glad to accept. This is especially true at the present time because there are more job openings than there are qualified veterinary technologists to take them. Salaries veterinary technicians earn also depend a great deal on their specializations and where they live. Jobs in small rural communities tend to pay less than jobs in larger metropolitan areas—but remember, it will cost you less to live in a rural area, so you should work wherever you truly want your home to be.

6

Training Animals to Work and Live with Humans

"Working animals," those who earn their keep by performing specific jobs, fall loosely into two categories: service and recreation. In both cases, animal trainers coach them so they can attain peak performance in their jobs.

Trainers demonstrate to an animal what it should do, make that behavior happen (using humane force if necessary), reward good results, and punish mistakes. This is a professional world that seems quite different when you shift your gaze from animal to animal. Equine trainers, those who specialize in breaking horses, employ very different strategies from those who train tigers or dogs. Their working environments will be very different, too. If you want to become a trainer, you will work with the animal of your choice—and there are plenty of choices to make in this field. Trainers work to break Thoroughbred horses with the goal of winning at the track or performing elegant dressage routines. Dog training specialists educate Seeing Eye dogs to guide the blind. They also equip other kinds of service dogs to perform certain household tasks for a wheelchair-bound owner, or brush up a new pup on a household's obedience routine. If you've ever seen the dolphins at Sea World or performing lions at Ringling Bros. and

Barnum & Bailey circus, you've probably guessed that the real star of the show was the trainer behind the exotic animals. Trainers, using their knowledge of conditioning, obedience commands, and motivational strategies, teach animals to support the endangered or physically challenged, to compete as animal contestants in sporting events such as races, and to dazzle circus and racetrack crowds. Animal wranglers, trainers who work in movie and television productions, can even coach an animal to stardom. Trainers use many different techniques, but their goal is always the same: to condition animals to live up to "best of breed" obedience standards and to fulfill their greatest potential. A common denominator among all good breeders is their desire to bring animals into line without injuring them or breaking their spirits.

Horse Trainers

Foremost among trainers are those who work with Thoroughbred horses. These highly skilled workers are so valued that they traditionally ask for—and receive—a percentage of a horse's winnings, instead of just a straight salary. For someone like Bill Mott, the trainer who worked with the champion Thoroughbred Cigar, this kind of arrangement can lead to earnings in the hundreds of thousands of dollars.

This high compensation makes sense when you understand that a horse trainer is really a master coach, carefully observing a Thoroughbred's strengths and weaknesses, likes and dislikes. Bill Mott took charge of four-year-old Cigar after a disappointing season. The horse had been training and running on grass. Mott thought Cigar might do better on a dirt track and switched him, with the result that he became a formidable champion whose winnings climbed into the millions of dollars. That one training decision may have been responsible for racing history.

There are almost as many training regimens as there are trainers, but typically, a trainer will direct a horse's nutritional and exercise programs, oversee boarding conditions, administer any necessary discipline, and devise incentives to encourage productive behaviors. Trainers will closely study a horse's "conformation," or body type, to see whether it will meet with greater success on the track, trail, or in a show arena. Then they carefully play to its strengths.

Horses often begin ground training very young. The trainer then decides whether a horse should be fed grass hay or alfalfa hay, grain or a calcium/magnesium combination, all depending on what jobs the animal will be doing (roping, jumping, performing, or racing). The trainer also will acquaint the horse with frightening objects it might encounter, such as ground poles. A horse and its trainer will prepare for a big race or performance in much the same way as an Olympic athlete and his or her coach. Trainers are careful to see that their horses are rested as well as exercised, rewarded as well as challenged. Trainers also are the ones to coax their horses into the gate, the metal structure that holds them in place until "And they're off!" signals that a race has begun. This procedure is so important that tracks such as Saratoga make Thoroughbreds pass a "gate test" before they are allowed to race. If the horse is destined for the show circuit rather than racing, trainers are the ones who offer treats and affection to horses after they've mastered intricate dressage movements and have obeyed all commands.

Training Animals to Work and Live with Humans

Trainers pick one aspect of their profession to focus on. Bill Mott is an example of a trainer at the top of the Thoroughbred racing game. Other trainers make a living preparing horses just for steeplechase races or equestrian competitions. Still others work with performance horses destined to entertain in the arenas of circuses, rodeos, and state and county fairs. Finally, trainers break "everyday" horses destined for practical work like trail riding and roundups on farms and ranches.

Salaries and Opportunities for Horse Trainers

Trainers of noncompetitive horses charge hourly rates or monthly fees, depending on the services they render. These fees can vary widely, depending on location, but a typical range would be $25-$55 per hour. Highly specialized trainers who work with hard-to-break or extremely valuable animals may charge over $100 per hour. Trainers make their own determinations about how high their rates will be. Their calculations factor in how much their local market can bear, their professional clout, and whether they are partner-trainers who must pay expenses out of their own pockets or contractors who keep 100 percent of their after-tax hourly fees. In some cases, trainers may become salaried employees for large corporate ranches or other businesses that use horses. In large cities and some pockets of the military, it is not uncommon to have a few mounted police (or troops) who train horses. These trainers are compensated at established civil service or military rates of pay. Their salaries generally begin in the mid-$20,000 range with benefits, though they can rise to a very good level with seniority.

Dog Trainers

The American Dog Trainers' Network (ADTN) estimates that although you can complete an initial professional training course in about four months, it takes from three to five years of intense, hands-on work to become an effective novice trainer.

Obedience Training

It may take as many as twenty years to become an acknowledged master of this demanding discipline, an expert who gives popular seminars, publishes, and speaks to obedience clubs. Although most families who acquire a new puppy read at least one training book, ADTN cautions strongly that anyone who wants to become a professional dog trainer should avoid correspondence courses. Even if a mail order course is expensive and offers "certification," the student trainer won't know if he or she is mishandling a dog unless an experienced coach is present to watch him or her work and to offer constructive criticism. If you are considering signing up for a training course but you're unsure about the reputation of the school you're looking at, you may want to contact the National Association of Dog Obedience Instructors or a veterinarian within the training school's area. Most professionals are willing to report if they've received substantial negative feedback on a training academy.

If you live near New York City, one of the best resources in the nation is the ASPCA's Animal Behavior Center, which has 1,200 square feet of dog training space and two new exam rooms. The center offers behavioral classes, puppy training, and agility training. In addition, the ASPCA is known for its "train the trainer" master classes, offered to veterinarians, doctoral candidates, and post-doctoral fellows in the clinical behavior of companion animals.

Trainers approved as professional teachers by the ADTN typically offer courses from two to four months in length. Expect to pay a tuition of at least $600–$750 per semester, with additional charges for distance learning materials. (Note: these are different from traditional correspondence courses, requiring at least some attendance in class.) Also, enter the profession with the expectation that you will be attending classes and seminars throughout your working life. It is very important to keep abreast of the newest conditioning methods if you hope to stay at the top of your game.

Robin Kovary, helpline director for the American Dog Trainers' Network, assembled the following traits she considers indispensable for a professional dog trainer. Match them against your own personal qualities to see if this business is a good fit for you.

A Good Trainer:
- Has lots of tools in his or her toolbox and knows how to use them well.
- Strives to learn as much as possible, from as many sources as possible.
- Knows there's always more to learn and keeps himself or herself up to date by attending seminars, workshops, and conferences as often as possible.
- Has a strong behavioral background.
- Has an open mind and loves dogs.
- Does not behave in an arrogant manner.
- Has a strong sense of ethics.
- Doesn't misrepresent himself or herself with bogus or misleading titles or credentials.

- Has patience and understands that anger and abuse (of any kind) have no place in dog training.
- Treats his or her students, both two- and four-legged, with respect and kindness. (Empathy, compassion, kinship, and encouragement toward one's students are essential when training dogs.)
- Has good teaching and handling skills.
- Has a good sense of humor.
- Is passionate about living and working with dogs.

SERVICE DOGS

Trainers who prepare dogs to support blind or wheelchair-bound humans make a tremendous difference in the overall quality of life for those who need assistance with everyday tasks. Careful, case-by-case instruction for these special dogs is essential. There are no easy shortcuts in service training, which represents a triple challenge, because trainers strive to ensure that dogs are warm and loving companions, housebroken and respectful of property, and that they are constant, predictable, and 100 percent reliable in fulfilling their assigned tasks. Why use dogs instead of other kinds of animals? They are the proper size to work alongside humans, they live for a long time and can support an owner for approximately eight years, and their high intelligence enables them to understand orders and to independently figure out what the best action is in any given situation. That way, if their owners are unable to communicate or unable to see traffic developments, the dogs will understand what needs to be done to get to a destination safely or to complete a household task.

SEEING EYE DOGS FOR THE BLIND

The Seeing Eye, America's preeminent guide school, works only with dogs who have been to preschool—or "puppy-garten." Over 750 volunteers in New Jersey, Pennsylvania, and Delaware provide early training to these dogs with a special destiny. Puppy raisers expose their young charges to stimuli like traffic, pavement, stores, and people—opportunities a kennel-raised dog would rarely get.[20] They also make sure that these dogs have a foundation of love and trust that will enable them to bond warmly with their blind owners. The friendship of these dogs is almost as important as their navigational help.

Early-stage training of a Seeing Eye dog is handled by a sighted person, but as soon as possible the blind owners partner with their new dogs to complete a demanding preparatory course. It's often said that these dogs are educated rather than trained, so they can make up their own minds about what to do whenever that becomes necessary. Maneuvers are designed to be as instructive for the blind human as they are for the dog companion. The blind must learn, through the use of the guiding stick, to sense when the dog is standing still, which cannot immediately be detected with just a strap. Over a course of weeks, the guide dog and owner become a skilled team, each highly sensitive to the other's concerns.

Very early in training, the owner assumes responsibility for all care and feeding, so the guide dog will look to him or her as the sole source of food and protection. That is why blind owners of guide dogs discourage friends and family from offering snacks.

[20] www.seeingeye.org/puppy.html.

Early trial runs are made through neighborhoods the dog already knows. Gradually, as the guide dog develops advanced navigational skills and sensitivity to traffic cues, the working area can expand. Completion of guide dog training, which takes about four months, is marked with a graduation celebration. Then training along the blind owner's usual routes in his or her hometown is the next step. Sometimes, when guide dogs reach old age, they are returned to the homes that cared for them as puppies to enjoy well-earned retirements.

TRAINING OTHER KINDS OF SERVICE DOGS

- **Service dogs** are versatile, assisting people with a wide range of disabilities, not just blindness. They are taught to do many things, including picking up dropped objects, pulling wheelchairs, predicting seizures, and helping with stability for those who have trouble walking. During instructional maneuvers, a training collar may be used. This type of collar is for control, never for the infliction of pain. Corrections are always made without injuring an animal. The entire point of the service dog's training cycle is to get lessons across with firmness, gentleness, and consistency—with a low-pitched, not angry voice, and a pat or other expression of approval whenever the dog obeys.

In the last decade, a new kind of training—"clicker" training, that uses a small toy clicker to provide a sound cue—has grown in popularity. In clicker obedience classes, trainers watch for the behavior that is wanted, mark the instant it happens with a click, then pay off with a treat. Treats may be food, affection, praise, or anything else the dog enjoys. The system was first used by dolphin trainers, who needed a way to condition behavior without using physical force.

Most service dogs undergo basic obedience training, just as any pet would, before they proceed to advanced training that will prepare them to work in a narrow specialty, such as mobility or sound sensitivity. These companion animals are permitted by law in all public places and are trained to travel on all forms of public transportation, including buses, trains, and subways. They are also taught to work in highly trafficked areas such as shopping malls. Canine Companions for Independence, a nonprofit organization serving the needs of the disabled, places hand-picked animals with qualified puppy raisers when they are about seven weeks of age. When they are about thirteen to eighteen months of age, they are returned to the CCI Training Institute for six months of intense training.

- **Dogs for the hearing impaired** are taught to alert their masters to the sounds of everyday life, such as doorbells, alarm clocks, telephones, smoke detectors, the cries of a baby, and other sound cues. When the dog hears a sound, it will jump on, or paw, its master to get attention—then lead its owner to the source of the sound. In some countries, Hearing Ear dogs are identified by a brightly colored collar and leash. The dog's attention must remain on its owner at all times and people are discouraged from petting a working dog while it's in uniform.[21]

---

[21] Hearing Ear Dogs of Canada.

- **Seizure-sensitive dogs** perform a wonderful, and somewhat mysterious, service by alerting epileptics and others who suffer from seizure disorders just before an attack occurs. The animals somehow sense when their masters are about to have a seizure. Though no one really understands exactly how the dogs know when a seizure is imminent, they provide enough of a warning for their human partners to arrange themselves safely. The dogs then function as guardians, staying close beside until their owners' seizures subside.

- **Skilled companion dogs** benefit humans with disabilities who need social, interactive, and functional help. These service dogs usually add to a paralytic's range of motion by retrieving objects, performing simple but essential chores, and obeying up to two dozen commands. The warmth and companionship these animals provide are as valuable as the household help they offer. Many of the disabled are isolated for up to eight hours per day, when family members or paid caregivers must be away from home. A friendly canine presence makes a crucial difference in the quality of their lives and states of mind.

Dogs and cats are also used as therapy animals, to provide emotional support and stimulus for patients in long-term care facilities and hospitals, and for children in day care centers. Judith Pickell, a breeder and trainer in Brownsburg, Indiana, who also works as a registered nurse, has employed animal therapy in her practice for the last twenty years. "Therapy animals cause people to stand when they didn't think they could and use their hands better because they want to hold or touch the dog," she says.[22]

> [About] dogs being taken to nursing homes and dogs as companion animals...People really respond much better than they do to humans. They know no dog is going to judge them and say, "Oh, that's disgusting." Dogs really do accept.—Jeffrey Masson

- **Search and rescue dogs, or SAR dogs,** make a life-or-death difference when they embark on humanitarian missions to locate survivors or missing bodies. The use of these dogs is nothing new; in Europe, they have led search and rescue operations for decades. After World War II, search and rescue dogs were used extensively to locate the casualties of battle and missing persons.

What enables a search and rescue dog to find missing humans? Each individual has skin, hair, and clothing particles and sweat and oil vapors that comprise a unique scent. These microscopic particles are detectable only to a canine's finely tuned nose.[23] Trainers condition their animals to follow scents in two ways. Tracking dogs are trained to follow the scent a person leaves on the ground. Scout dogs, often trained by the military, find persons or bodies from scents carried through the air. A well-trained dog can smell and locate a person as much as a quarter-mile away. Experienced search dog trainers and handlers work with

[22] *Indianapolis Star,* Sept. 30, 1997.
[23] ABSAROKA Search Dogs, www.wtp.net/ASDK9SAR.html.

their animals to track persons lost in rubble from disasters, ice, snow, and water.[24]

Training for search and rescue dogs is very challenging, and professional trainers who condition them must be prepared for some unpleasantness. In avalanche training, for example, volunteers are buried in snow caves. Dogs track the scent and are taught to dig down to the buried person. In wilderness handling, areas are sectioned off, with each dog bearing responsibility for its own bordered sector. Night training is critical because searches after dark are relatively successful; lost persons move around less then, which means that scenting conditions improve.

Most search and rescue dog handlers attend training exercises at least twice a month. These are authentic stagings of disaster scenarios in the wild, near water, or on snow and ice. The American Rescue Dog Association, established in 1972, modeled standards and training methods that came to be used around the nation. Each ARDA unit must pass rigorous field examinations periodically.

Search and rescue dog trainers do not undertake their work in hopes of making a lot of money. Their assignments are almost always volunteer. In fact, the cost of boarding, training, and veterinary care for each SAR dog is over $1,500 per year, so it's accurate to say that these trainers do their work for love, not money.

ANTITERRORIST DOGS (BOMB SNIFFERS)

The Pentagon's Working Dog Program manages 1,394 dogs in the U.S. Army, Air Force, Navy, and Marine Corps. In unstable parts of the world, these animals

---

[24]German Shepherd Search Dogs of Washington State, www.gssd.org/GSSD/gssdinfo.htm.

sniff out explosives and patrol areas surrounding American troops. They also regularly help U.S. Customs officials find contraband along the U.S. borders and in major airports and seaports.

Antiterrorist dogs are selected for their stable temperaments. They are also screened for hip and joint problems and the ability to adapt to an environment with lots of upheaval.

They are acquired for about $4,000 per dog, and usually $30,000 is spent to train each working dog and its human handler. About 65 percent of all potential "sniffers" are rejected. Because of increasing demand for their services all over the world, branches of the military are now considering whether to start their own breeding programs. Military trainers already are responsible for instilling high level "sniffing" skills into these intelligent and courageous dogs, as well as conditioning them to obey orders instantly. The hope is that breeding on military bases will save both money and time.[25]

Training Performance Animals

The animal rights group PETA (People for the Ethical Treatment of Animals) has targeted a group of circuses and live animal shows it accuses of not meeting minimal standards for humane treatment of performing animals. In fact, the treatment of all performing animals has come under close scrutiny in the past decade. It's no wonder: Circuses are big business. Ringling Bros. and Barnum & Bailey circuses are enjoyed by more than 10 million paying guests per year. In an attempt to guarantee the humane treatment of performance, especially

---

[25]*Chicago Sun Times*, May 29, 1999.

circus, animals, the U.S. Department of Agriculture reviews circuses for compliance on maintaining veterinary records, providing sufficient space, providing safe and comfortable transport, and exercising animal performers, among other concerns. Animal rights activists have accused circus and show trainers of pushing animals to exhaustion, keeping them in unsanitary conditions, and conditioning them with cruel and painful obedience cues.

The best entertainment animal trainers are consistent and kind to their charges, however, because in the long run, the animals will work harder and give a more spirited performance if they want to please the trainer. Animals like lions, tigers, and bears can turn dangerous very quickly if they become angry at a trainer, so the best workers in this highly skilled profession stay on an even keel. Circus wildlife training is one area where apprentices are apt to learn from master trainers in a controlled environment, or once in a while in special circus schools. Part of the problem with inhumane circus training has been the lack of monitoring and the dominance of the profession by older trainers. As younger trainers, who are more attuned to animal rights, move into the spotlight, improvements can be expected. Their job will be a big one because not only must they condition the animals to perform, but they must monitor the nutrition, housing accommodations, and physical development of their animal charges.

You couldn't expect to find two more loving performance trainers than Galina and Vitaly Sashin, who work for a small Jerusalem circus. Their stars are their beloved pets as well as their performers. Each night the Sashins watch television in bed "as a family" with all of their poodles. The dogs are hugged, bathed, and pampered at home, where Galina first trains them by teaching them to dance to recorded music. Because they are natural mimics, the poodles pick up new choreography and tricks easily. The dogs don't rehearse every day, but they rehearse intensively before a performance. After their work is done, they live it up at home with a reward-dinner of kasha, apples, bananas, rice, cooked vegetables, and occasionally chicken or meat.[26] Galina trains the dogs to heed her voice commands and finger snapping. She credits her training success to the breed, and says that while poodles are not quite human beings, they are close to humans in terms of intelligence.

Charly Bauman, senior animal trainer of Ringling Bros. and Barnum & Bailey, gets top billing in his circus's official program. He works with tigers, training them as young as nine or ten months of age. "I treat the tigers like a kindergarten class," he says. "When they're playing, I study them to see which ones are capable of doing things and which ones are the troublemakers. I weed out the troublemakers early because later on, when they get big, all they're going to do is look for fights with other tigers."[27] It takes twelve months of training, every day twice a day, to train a new troupe of tigers from scratch. It then takes an additional year to fine-tune a new tiger act.

When working on a new trick, Bauman puts a piece of meat on the end of a stick, leads the tiger through whatever movement is wanted, then rewards him or her with the meat. After a few months, it is no

[26]Fishkoff, Sue, *Jerusalem Post*, Dec. 15, 1995.
[27]Klemesrud, Judy, *New York Times*, Apr. 16, 1982.

longer necessary to use the meat; the stick and his or her voice are sufficient cues.

Bauman also has trained bears, which he says are much more dangerous than tigers because they give no warning of attack. It's also hard to distract a bear once he's on top of the trainer, whereas a tiger can be distracted by a yell from outside the cage.

7

Breeding Animals Is Big Business

Animal breeding, or husbandry, is a global enterprise undertaken by giant corporations, small businesses, and individuals. The goal shared by all is to monitor reproduction so that specific desirable traits of an animal will surface when it is bred. This is a field that was highly professionalized in the last century. Many land grant and agricultural colleges, in particular, began offering degree programs with various concentrations in animal husbandry. Cazenovia College in New York, for example, began offering a certificate program in equine reproductive management. The certificate was designed to complement an associate's or bachelor's degree. Typically, a student in the associate degree program in stable and farm management will decide to remain an additional year to complete work on a certificate, or a bachelor of science candidate will gain certification as part of program studies. Before a student is finished, he or she will have been exposed to breeding lab design and management, breeding and foaling management, equine anatomy and physiology, and even equine promotion, marketing, and sales. In other colleges nationwide, there are certificate and degree programs that focus on other kinds of livestock, poultry, and even aquaculture, the breeding of fish and other marine life.

The work animal breeders do has many practical applications. In the future, human beings who desperately need organ transplants may heal with the help of organs from pigs especially bred for that purpose. Food animals are already scientifically bred to guarantee more meat yield per animal. Racehorses are bred for classic conformity. Dog and cat breeders encourage specific temperament and physical qualities in animals destined to compete in championship arenas. They also produce pedigreed offspring for pet markets. Finally, animal breeders work to provide specimens for laboratory studies—so that, for example, there will be an ample supply of a specific kind of rat needed to test a cancer-fighting drug.

In food-animal markets, over 900,000 units of semen from beef sires were sold in the United States last year, and over 2 million units of custom frozen beef semen were sold. The top four breeds represented in this latter market were Angus, Simmental, Red Angus, and Polled Hereford, all top steak- and chop-producing animals. In addition to breeding from frozen semen, breeders preserve valuable animal characteristics by quick-freezing embryos (animal eggs penetrated by sperm), though this process works well only among selected species.[28]

Animal breeding companies are also extremely interested in the science of cloning so they can duplicate their best animals. A limited amount of cloning can speed the reproductive process along, bringing the meat or milk yield of an average cow or sheep closer to that of the best of breed.[29] The ethical concerns that

[28] *Farmers Journal*, Feb. 28, 1997.
[29] *Farmers Weekly*, Feb. 28, 1997.

Breeding Animals Is Big Business

surround human cloning are largely absent in animal cloning. Profitable businesses such as Zoogen, Inc., and SmithKline Beecham, Inc., have become successful by providing genetic data management and analysis for animal breeders, who then use it to make investment and species reproduction decisions.

Companion animal breeding also has become a major business, though it is one area where most consumers would prefer to deal with a smaller "mom and pop" operation. In recent years, horror stories of negligent "puppy mills" have received widespread publicity, forcing authorities to impose higher breeding standards and more frequent inspections on these businesses. Many states also impose taxes and surcharges on pet breeders. The best operators don't breed any more animals than they can attend to and keep clean and well nourished. They carefully breed companion animals to type—that is, with the goal of producing desirable characteristics of a particular strain—and wait at least eighteen months or until the second season for females and twelve months for males to mature. Only then can they be reasonably sure of the health of the parent animals and their babies.

One of the most famous and highly regarded breeding businesses in America is run as a small cottage industry by an order of Russian Orthodox monks in New Skete, New York. Their method is so admired that they were asked to describe it in two popular books. The monks work with German shepherds exclusively and have a reputation for breeding dogs that result in especially sweet-tempered and obedient puppies. There is a two-year waiting list for a New Skete shepherd—and these pups usually sell for about $1,000.

If you're interested in animal breeding as a pathway to riches, be warned. Breeders can earn adequate supplementary incomes, but in many cases, expenses cancel out profits. Puppy and kitten breeders pay large sums for registered sires and bitches, the clinical term used to describe the female dog. In addition, they must pay taxes and kennel club fees and buy high quality vitamins and food. Routine visits to the veterinarian, injections, and ear- and tail-docking for some breeds increase costs further. If there is a problem with delivering a litter, the animal doctor must be called in at considerable cost. When a puppy or kitten is offered for several hundred or a thousand dollars, it sounds like a lot of money—but the breeder may not make that much when his or her time and care are factored in and added to operating expenses.

8

The Boarding Business: Simple Pet-Sitting to Luxury Pet Hotels

Pet owners usually can't, or don't want to, stay home all the time. If they travel on business or take a vacation, not all hotels, motels, and bed-and-breakfast establishments are pet-friendly. In these cases, it's less trouble for the owner, and usually kinder for the pet, to use the services of a professional kennel, boarding establishment, or pet-minder.

Many animal clinics offer boarding services as a way to generate extra fees. They will keep sick animals overnight and add a boarding surcharge to the treatment bill. This is a particularly good idea if your pet is being neutered or has had emergency surgery. The veterinarian or veterinary technologist will keep a watchful eye on Fido in the medical recovery room, then deal with any postsurgical complications that may arise. Vacationers also like to leave their pets with a vet because they can take advantage of vaccination update programs and special grooming packages while their animals board. Depending on location, typical boarding fees run from $10 to $20 per night in most American cities, excluding optional services such as grooming or vaccinations.

Some nonclinical boarding establishments have gotten quite elaborate and offer an almost spalike atmosphere for pampered pets. In the United Kingdom, the Triple A Animal Hotel and Care Center employs thirty-seven people and provides accommodations for up to 300 animals—mainly cats, dogs, and horses. Pet owners pay about $25 per day for luxury "rooms." There is an aerobic center where pets can work out by climbing a complicated apparatus, a pet swimming pool, and a communal lounge area where television-loving cats and dogs can watch their favorite shows. Each pet gets eight walks per day. A variety of grooming services are also provided. Any staff member who joins Triple A is asked to continue his or her education in basic animal care. The operation has become so successful that its owners are considering franchising it.[30]

In Webster, Texas, Trisha Reed—who formerly managed an animal hospital—owns the Barkington Inn and Pet Resort, where room rates range from $12 a night to $25 for theme-decorated luxury rooms. Each "guest" receives a daily change of linens, room service, and a bedtime snack. The business is grossing $26,000 per month and employs twenty caregivers.[31]

One of the newest trends in pet care is not to board at all, but rather to hire a pet-sitter to come directly to your residence. This is particularly useful when dealing with older animals, who tend to get set in their ways and may be frightened by confinement in an unfamiliar kennel. Pets continue life as usual in the comfort of their own homes, with the visiting pet-sitter coming by at agreed-upon intervals to exercise the animal, freshen its food and water, and extend a little love and

---

[30]*People Management*, Dec. 24, 1998.

[31]Hansen, Susan, *Citation*, Sept. 1999.

companionship. Fees for this kind of service range from free (with neighbors exchanging this kind of help) to $50 per day, depending on location, kinds and numbers of pets, and additional services that are requested. In 1993, the National Association of Professional Pet Sitters established itself as a nonprofit membership organization. Members must sign the NAPPS Code of Ethics when they join, and an advisory board of veterinarians, trainers, and nutritionists provides advice on animal welfare. This group provides a certification program as well as conferences that educate members on insurance requirements, cooperative programs, and how to give the best service to their stay-at-home clients.

9

Animal Makeovers: The Groomer's World

It's estimated that there are 6,000 pets for every animal grooming business operating today. There are shortages of skilled animal groomers in many urban areas; in some big city newspapers, there are upward of twenty jobs for groomers posted each week.

How to Become an Animal Groomer

If you choose a career in animal grooming, you can anticipate that your business and profits will expand in the future. This is an excellent opportunity for someone who loves working with animals but isn't fond of academic study, since most pet groomers take training courses that usually last from just ten to eighteen weeks. The best groomers make a point of taking continuing education courses to keep abreast of new developments and to work toward master groomer or master stylist credentials. Once you've graduated from a pet grooming academy, there will be opportunities to go to work in kennels, salons, mobile vans, veterinary clinics, and larger pet stores' grooming departments. Vocational licensing is not required in this field (though it has become a hot topic and is under consideration in several states), but it is a good idea to go through the process of certification because you'll learn more and the credential will lend some cachet to your new business. It also should be of help in the job hunting process, if you choose to gain experience as an employee rather than as a business owner. Information about certification can be gained from the following agencies:

Companion Animal Hygienist (CAH)	World Wide Pet Supplies Association	1-818-447-2222
National Certified Master Groomer (NCMG)	National Dog Groomers Association of America	1-724-962-2711
Certified Master Groomer (CMG)	International Professional Groomers	1-800-258-4765 (fax)
Certified Canine Cosmetologist (CCC)	International Society of Canine Cosmetologists	1-972-414-9715

Numbers from petgroomer.com

Is Animal Grooming for You?

If you want to make it in this field, there are some basic questions you'll need to ask yourself. For starters, do you truly like animals, or are you sometimes afraid of them? Are you allergic to any of them? Are you willing to take inoculations such as a tetanus shot to guarantee your safety on the job? Will you be able to remain a good sport when your canine clients bark nonstop, or when you must spend prolonged time in a warm and humid bathing area? How do you feel about cleaning up animal wastes—can you cheerfully regard this as just part of the job? Can you pick up pets that may weigh as much as 150 pounds, or do you have back problems or suffer from repetitive stress injuries? The motions of brushing, combing, and lifting for hours every day can aggravate conditions such as carpal tunnel syndrome, so you'll need to have reasonable stamina and a clean bill of health from your doctor before you commit to this kind of work.

You'll need to be artistic, but with the willingness and ability to copy formula cuts. This is especially important for dogs competing in kennel shows, as they are evaluated on whether they conform to classic looks established for their breeds. You'll also need some knowledge of health care and safety procedures, as animals can suffer just as humans can when they are exposed to caustic or irritating grooming agents.

If you put up your own shingle, you'll want to have a sound business plan and an understanding of billing, accounting, and marketing procedures. Your state's Bureau for Small Business Development can be of help here. Trade magazines such as *Groomer to Groomer* and *Pet Stylist* also can be of help. You'll probably need to work with an accountant to set up a system of recordkeeping so that you'll have a solid understanding of your profits and losses at tax time. Finally, if your state requires you to collect sales receipts or receipts taxes on services (not all states do), you'll need to learn how to do that, too.[32]

Although the public tends to think of pet grooming parlors as storefront operations, some innovative groomers have taken their small businesses on the road. Lynn Chadney, owner of The Ruff Trade, a mobile grooming business for pets, cruises the streets of Los Angeles in a customized vehicle that includes a bathtub, blow-dryer, vacuum, and products such as shampoos and flea-killing concoctions. For each

[32]http://www.petgroomer.com.

appointment, she parks in a client's driveway, retrieves the pet and gives it a bath, a trim, and a "pet-icure." Her charge per animal is $40, and her clientele has grown into the hundreds.[33]

Although you will not have to become certified unless you want to, virtually all pet groomers attend commercial animal grooming schools, where typically they undergo from 300–550 hours of training. The more hours of training, the likelier the student will be to gain complete mastery of the art. Madeline's Institute of Pet Grooming in Santa Clara, California, is a highly regarded institution that offers a thirteen-week, 528-hour professional pet groomer curriculum for $3,600. Madeline's adds a $75 registration fee and charges students for a grooming toolbox, which costs about $995 wholesale. An advanced pet groomer seminar is offered for $750 for eighty hours. There is also a professional pet bather course that lasts 144 hours and costs $900, plus $75 registration and a $595 toolbox fee. Schools like Madeline's emphasize hands-on training for students. Industry standard-keepers caution applicants to tour schools they are considering, to insist upon a clear understanding of tuition and fees (many schools offer payment plans), and to try to avoid situations where classmates have to share pets in grooming laboratories or may not get a chance to work on all breeds.

---

[33] Cardenas, Jose, *Los Angeles Times*, February 16, 2000.

10

Pet Store Owners and Marketers

Owning or managing a specialty store is one way to enjoy the company of animals and animal lovers as you earn a living—but be aware that this field is changing dramatically. It's sad but true: Small mom-and-pop pet stores are losing ground to conglomerate superstores, Internet businesses, and even specialty corners of giant supermarkets. In the past, pet store owners usually were animal lovers who decided to go into a business that focused on their interests. While this still happens, more M.B.A.'s (Master of Business Administration graduates) are treating pet sales and supplies as the profitable business it is, with one-stop shopping that serves all of a pet's needs. In other words, the focus is moving from animals themselves to inventories of "pet support" items like food, nonprescription medicines, toys, beds, treats, grooming supplies, and hardware such as specialty nail clippers.

THE INDEPENDENT PET STORE

In smaller American communities, however, the independent pet store still has an honored place. Ron and Michelle Cook run All Star Pets, a 2,000-square-foot store in Canon City, Colorado. They feel that the store (their second) is a success because they carry specialty foods like Hills Science Diet for dogs and cats, as well as "feeder" animals for predator-pets. This would include mice and rats for hungry snakes, and mealworms and crickets for lizards and other reptiles. They specialize in saltwater fish, but also carry freshwater fish, turtles, frogs, newts, lizards, geckos, chameleons, iguanas, snakes, hamsters, gerbils, guinea pigs, rabbits, mice, and rats.[34]

Frank Cramer runs four regional pet stores, each located in a thriving mall. He reports that his upstate New York business increased 12 percent last year, probably due to the stores' emphasis on superior nutrition and employees' caring, hands-on attitude with owners who run into problems with their pets.

The advantage of owning a small pet shop is that your interaction with pet owners and their animals becomes very personal. You get to know all the veterinarians, breeders, and trainers in your area. It's possible to make a good living from such a business, particularly if the shop you've set up is in a well-to-do neighborhood. Even if you don't get rich, you'll experience the satisfaction of placing pets in responsible homes and following up with recommendations on diet, training, and other aspects of pet ownership. As with grooming businesses, if you want to open a small pet store, the most important step will be to write a business plan that covers everything from A to Z. You'll need a financial strategy, a promising location, market analysis, and a balanced inventory to get started. When you're starting your own store, it's a good first step to get suggestions from groups like the chamber of commerce and the retired executives service corps. You'll receive many helpful ideas—and they're free.

---

[34]Tracy, Darcy, *Pueblo Chieftain*, Mar. 6, 2000.

Stores like the Cooks', however, are beginning to be crowded-out by big-money corporations. In the year 2001, total annual spending on household pets will reach $28.5 billion, according to the American Pet Products Manufacturers' Association. Though much of that will be spent for veterinary services, most of it will go to large and elaborate pet superstores.

THE PET SUPERSTORE

These superstores are working hard to win your business.[35] In the early 1980s, supermarkets sold 95 percent of all dog and cat food. Ten years later, 89 percent of dog food sales and 29 percent of "by the pound" pet food sales were rung up by the pet superstores, which are dedicated solely to pets and pet products.[36] Patrons of these stores tend to be well-off financially, with about 40 percent having a $40,000 annual income or higher. They tell pollsters that they appreciate the convenience of features such as once-a-week vaccination clinics and semiautomatic dog washes.

If you want to get involved in this kind of operation, the best thing you can do is work for a superstore after school or for limited hours on weekends. See how you like it. Your first chores probably will be to work with stock, as dog and cat food, kitty litter, and bird seed must be restocked once a week. Rawhide bones, milk bones, play balls, and veterinary remedies also need to be restocked periodically. Becoming familiar with products, store inventory, and the needs of customers will provide a great education. It's possible to move to a management position simply by demonstrating your

[35]Adams, Liz, *Marketing*, Feb. 16, 1998.
[36]Nielsen Consumer Information Services.

commitment and reliability. Usually, these stores ask for a bachelor's degree with an emphasis on business as an entry-level management requirement. Pet superstores also like to hire two-year veterinary technology graduates. The field is wide open, and if you are eager to learn, enjoy working with animals and people, and think you'd like the security of a corporate job, a career in superstore sales may be right for you.

A new marketing trend that may eclipse even the superstores is direct sales of pet supplies on the Internet. You won't enjoy direct contact with animals in this line of work, but a knowledge of pets and the food, grooming aids, drugs, and toys they prefer will help you get your foot in the door. Big retail businesses such as Pet Food Express, which is headquartered in San Leandro, California, have launched national "e-tailing" sites. Their plan is to keep their sixteen stores in business but to cater to pet owners over the Internet as well.

11

Zoologists Classify the Animal Kingdom

Have you ever owned an aquarium or ant farm, or enjoyed collecting butterflies or other insects? Do you like peering into microscopes to study living cells as they swim about and divide? Would you be thrilled to discover a species no one had ever identified before? If so, the profession of zoologist might be of interest to you.

WHAT ZOOLOGISTS DO

The main task of these scientists is to study and classify members of the animal kingdom, including marine life and tiny animals like parasites. Often zoologists will specialize in one category of animals. Herpetologists, for example, focus just on reptiles and amphibians. Usually these people work at colleges and universities or for special institutions devoted to work such as preserving endangered species. But sometimes they do what their job title suggests: take jobs in zoos. This is a hard field to break into because there are more zoology graduates than available zoo jobs, but if you love the field and work diligently to find a position, you can succeed in finding one. Once you're employed, you'll be devoting far more energy to the job than zoologists did in the past, since you will be making sure that animals are comfortable in habitats created to resemble

Zoologists Classify the Animal Kingdom

their homes in the wild. Modern zoos bear little resemblance to the cages with iron bars that made resident animals look like prison inmates. Great care is taken, instead, to provide vegetation and an environment that will encourage completely natural behavior. Zoologists who work as zookeepers now understand that animals who are happy in their man-made abodes live longer and respond more affectionately to their caregivers.

A group of zookeeping professionals established a nonprofit volunteer organization, the American Association of Zoo Keepers, in 1967 in San Diego, California—home of the world-famous zoo. Their goal is to promote professionalism in their work by educating staff members in the most current techniques of captive exotic animal care. Membership is currently at 2,800 and includes staff members working at all levels, not just those with zoology or other scientific degrees. This group sponsors seminars and publications on crisis management, zoonotic diseases, diet and enrichment, and animal behavior. Members from all fifty states, five Canadian provinces, and twenty-four foreign countries regularly communicate to exchange zoo and animal-related information.

Dr. David Hillis, who works at the University of Texas as a zoology professor, provides a fascinating example of how someone becomes a zoologist and establishes himself or herself as a leader in the field. Hillis was already catching lizards and snakes in the African jungle at the age of six. In his early twenties, he discovered a new type of frog. Hillis discovered a new species of snake in Ecuador after a landslide blocked the road he was travelling and tossed rocks into his car. With single-minded focus, he continued his search. His special interest, evolutionary biology, gives scientists a glimpse of where species come from and how they develop. Recently, the MacArthur Foundation awarded Hillis a $295,000 "genius grant" to be paid over five years and to be used any way he likes.[37] He is now considered one of the most distinguished zoologists in the world, but his career path was not that different from anyone else's. He turned a childhood interest and adult passion into a moneymaking enterprise through a combination of advanced education, hard work, persistence, and careful documentation of his research findings.

THE INS AND OUTS OF ZOOLOGY JOBS

Although jobs in zoos and wildlife preserves are relatively scarce, there are some zoology jobs with growth potential. Parasitology, the study of organisms that use other plants and animals as hosts, has become a rapidly expanding field. Parasites cause disease in humans, plants, and animals. They also corrupt food sources, which is dangerous because in some parts of the world, an explosive human growth rate means that there are already inadequate supplies of wholesome food. The need is great for zoologists who can use their knowledge of parasites in public health, agriculture, aquaculture, and the pharmaceutical industries.

Educational Requirements and Salaries

Zoology is a field where you probably will need to go to graduate school after college. Although some good jobs are available to graduates with a B.S. degree, most zoologists have a Ph.D. or an M.D. degree. Almost all

---

[37] *Houston Chronicle,* June 23, 1999.

zoologists conduct research, publish, and teach at the college level. For these kinds of activities, it's usually necessary to have the terminal, or highest, degree awarded in your major area of study. Expect to take an entry-level job in the low- to-mid-twenties, then slowly increase your rate of pay according to seniority. Senior faculty members can earn $85,000 or more, and many supplement their salaries with research grants, publications, or by teaching extra classes in summer school. Industrial zoologists usually start out in the low-$30,000 range, then increase their pay incrementally through merit and seniority awards each year. Zoologists who work for nonprofit foundations vary widely in salary, depending on how well a foundation is endowed. Some of the better jobs in this field are civil service positions that credit employees for advanced degrees and meritorious performance. These jobs can start in the mid-$30,000 to mid-$50,000 range. As with any job, the cost of living in an area affects salary level.

1

Marine Biologists: Getting into the Swim

If you are fascinated by oceans and waterways and the creatures that live in them, then marine biology—the study of aquatic life—may be for you. This is a graduate-level pursuit, so the best way to prepare is to take a strong bachelor's degree program in general biology or a related science.

How to Go About Being a Marine Biologist

You can get a technologist's job with a master's degree, but these days, if you hope to direct your own research, you'll probably need a Ph.D. If you wind up working for a university, as many marine biologists do, you'll be teaching as well as researching. Your hard work will pay off with a job that permits travel to scenic waterways and interactions with smart and interesting people. If you've ever seen any of the three films or seventy television specials made by Jacques Cousteau, you've already had a glimpse into just how exciting and mysterious the life of the marine biologist can be. Cousteau, though controversial, was one of the most popular and successful marine biologists ever. Interestingly, he was trained in the navy, rather than in a university doctoral program. But that was many years ago, before the job market became so competitive.

Marine Biologists: Getting into the Swim

You'd think marine biologists would always work in and around water, but that's not necessarily true. If you're studying populations of fish around a coral reef, be prepared for lots of scuba diving. Believe it or not, though, many of these scientists do their jobs in landlocked laboratories and never get wet.

The wide range of jobs loosely clustered under the heading of "marine biology" includes salt water and freshwater testing, evolutionary research, environmental protection, species preservation—just about any scientific activity you can name. Marine biologists also work in fisheries, aquariums, government agencies, and for nonprofit research foundations. Their focus may be on whales or dolphins, or microscopic life forms that can't be seen with the naked eye. Recent postings on the American Fisheries Society home page included jobs for a hatchery manager, environmental water resources scientist, and aquatic ecologist.

Educational Requirements and Salaries

Although it's a plus if your undergraduate program of study includes some marine biology, this is not a requirement. Any college with a good science program will do. Your college years will be a time to strengthen your powers of observation and analysis, and you can do this with most majors. Take all the science and math you can. If you can get a summer job assisting a marine biologist or oceanographer with his or her work, this will be even more valuable than taking classes. Be prepared for two years of master's degree study, and another six years of work on your Ph.D. Your earnings will be about the same as a zoologist's. If you teach, expect your first teaching salary to be in the high

$20,000 range, or the $30,000 range if your employer is well endowed. The Scripps Institution of Oceanography states that a graduate student earns about $12,500 per year, and a new Ph.D. earns about $25,000. Most biologists with Ph.D.'s earn in the $40,000–$50,000 range and beyond.

13

Animal Adoption Workers Provide Love and Homes for Unwanted Pets

When is professional-level animal care *not* a career? You won't receive a salary when you work to find adoptive homes for abandoned animals. But many committed volunteers give the gift of their time and ideas to local shelters and animal protection societies. They've learned that the rewards of giving a second chance to strays can't be measured in dollars and cents.

According to the American Society for the Prevention of Cruelty to Animals, some five million homeless cats and dogs are euthanized (legally put to sleep) each year in community shelters. There are up to ten million stray animals in the United States at any given time.[38]

Why Animals Are Given Up

Some of the most compassionate animal caregivers anywhere are the workers who do everything in their power to find homes for these abandoned strays. Animals are given up by their owners for many reasons: They no longer can afford the time and money it takes to care for a pet, an animal has littered and the resulting puppies and kittens can't easily be placed in homes,

---

[38] *Tampa Tribune*, Oct. 16, 1999.

or sometimes animals become separated from their owners. Mixed-breed dogs and cats are often passed along to shelters in favor of the pedigreed—a real shame, as mixed breeds are some of the healthiest and most intelligent pets around, since they haven't been over-bred from a single gene pool.

ASPCA Volunteers and Adoption Workers

Anyone fond of animals who can make a commitment to regular training and service is welcome to join the local ASPCA chapter or community shelter. Volunteers typically get to groom, clean, and assess animals for adoption potential. They have plenty of chances to cuddle and exercise them, too. In fact, if you think you might want to become a veterinarian or veterinary technician, there is no better way to see if you're really cut out for the work than to volunteer at a shelter.

Adoption workers have one of the more stressful volunteer jobs around, because it's so hard to see unwanted animals euthanized or passed over. Most shelters have detailed orientations, and some, like the Nebraska Humane Society, require volunteers to attend the screening of a film that addresses euthanasia from an abandoned dog's point of view. This helps workers deal with the inevitable emotional fallout when an animal they've become attached to can't find a home.

As common as euthanasia is, all over the country animal rights activists and shelter volunteers are working more aggressively than ever to identify homes for strays, precisely so healthy and loving animals won't have to be put down. At Maddie's Adoption Center in San Francisco, strays receive free behavior therapy, grooming services, workouts with a trainer, and high protein cuisine to make them more adoptable. Pinellas County in Florida asked its ASPCA shelter to add evening hours, so jobholders could pick out a pet without losing time in the office. Many local television stations now offer "pet of the week" segments, with promising results. Shopping malls, libraries, fairgrounds, pet superstores, and community festivals frequently sponsor adoption clinics. In San Diego, a particularly animal-loving city with a fine zoo, when county supervisors meet each week, they introduce an adoptable animal after the pledge of allegiance and before the politicking begins. According to the San Diego Union-Tribune, this strategy has worked 100 percent of the time. Animals up for adoption are then placed on display at the county administration building, where they serve as silent advocates to get a new central animal shelter built.

Also in San Diego, there is a "Santa Claws" adoption clinic following the city's Christmas parade; adoptive "parents" get a free photo with Santa and their new pet. At PetSmart adoption clinics, families are able to select a pet, pay a fee, and make arrangements for vaccinations and spaying or neutering, all in a few minutes' time.

Adoption workers frequently get involved in neutering drives because the least painful and most effective solution to the problem of abandoned animals is birth control. These days, most shelters refuse to finalize a placement until the adoptive family agrees to neutering. They have also learned to be wary of impulsive adoptions around holidays like Christmas; many refuse to let an animal go home within a holiday week. Their goal is for all placements to be thought through carefully and completely, so that the animals involved have a realistic chance of bonding with their new families and finding permanent homes.

Adoption and the Internet

The United Kingdom was one of the first countries to move the adoption of strays into the Internet era. UK Animal Rescuers launched one of the earliest and most comprehensive placement sites on the Internet.[39] This society provides a comprehensive directory to every adoption and animal welfare center in the country as well as photographic "personal ads" for hard-to-place cats and dogs, most often those who have been without homes for a year or more. Before each animal is fostered out, it gets a complete physical examination including vaccinations. In addition, its new owner must be reviewed favorably by trained Rescuers staff and pay a fee of about $75. Members of the public who want to help animals but do not have the necessary time or space for a personal adoption are encouraged to become sponsors of strays who can't find a home. It's possible to enter a credit card number to make an instant donation to the society—a procedure the ASPCA has been quick to follow.

I am frequently asked, how can you stand to spend so much time in a shelter? The truth is—I enjoyed it. What people don't realize is that there are numerous pleasures in shelter work. Socializing the animals, helping them to make it through difficult transitions between owners, just giving a dog the right haircut or a bath can make all the difference. I remember a badly matted cocker spaniel who came into the shelter after a long stray period. The poor little dog was filthy, hungry, and scared; she didn't come forward in her cage for several

---

[39] www.animalrescuers.co.uk.

ANIMAL ADOPTION WORKERS

days. Then Paul Beckers, a shelter volunteer, sat in the dog's cage for almost an hour. That was how long it took before she decided it was safe to crawl into his lap and begin to open up. Paul named her Lilly. She was subsequently groomed, spayed, and placed in a new home in less than a week. The greatest reward of my shelter work is seeing a dog or cat go home.

—Elizabeth Hess, author of Lost and Found *(Harcourt Brace)*

Educational Requirements and Salaries

There are no minimal educational requirements for adoption volunteers, but skills are important. Good interpersonal relations, record-keeping abilities, telephone manners, and even some technical background may be necessary, as some shelters now offer animals for adoption on public access television or the Web. Salaries range from low for volunteer coordinators, those staff members who schedule the training and duty rotation of the volunteer corps, to nothing for the helpers themselves. But the great feeling you'll get from a job well done will provide significant emotional rewards—as well as years of happiness for the animals you place.

14

Saving the Whales and Other Animals

If you are concerned about saving the whales, the American bald eagle, the peregrine falcon, or other endangered creatures, you might want to consider working in animal conservation. People who use the job title "animal conservationist" actually begin these careers with a variety of credentials. Some of their occupations include wildlife biologist, general biologist, educator, engineer, real estate specialist, ranger, outdoor recreation specialist, and management analyst. To succeed in an animal conservation career, you should be appreciative of the natural world. You should like science, enjoy adventure and the outdoors, and have a knack for problem solving. You'll need to be patient, too, for participating in a census of an endangered species is painstaking labor, and working to replenish an animal population can take many years. Even if you wind up working on a project in an office, following the bureaucratic ins and outs of the project will require your closest attention. One missed step can set a conservation project back weeks or even months.

Endangered Species
The United States government, individual states, and private foundations work hard to keep endangered

animal species from becoming extinct. Congress passed the Endangered Species Law in 1966. This law restricted endangered lists to native animals and provided some means for their protection. In 1969, the Endangered Species Conservation Act provided additional protection to animals in danger of worldwide extinction. The Departments of the Interior, Agriculture, and Defense were directed to protect listed species and whenever possible, to preserve their habitats. The Endangered Species Act of 1973 strengthened the two earlier provisions even further and offered federal matching grants to states. Because each one of the United States is eligible to receive these grants, if you want to work in this field, chances are good that you'll have the opportunity to do so in your own backyard. Animal conservationists routinely advise agencies, builders, developers, and individuals to keep commercial projects from disrupting endangered creatures on their natural turf.

U.S. Fish and Wildlife Service

Probably the largest employer of people who work to protect endangered animals is the U.S. Fish and Wildlife Service, which keeps more than 7,500 men and women representing a diverse range of specialties, professions, and backgrounds on the payroll. The process they use is called species recovery, and it can be very challenging because even experts don't always know why a class of animals is in decline. Service employees oversee independent consultants who create and put recovery plans into action. These plans are aimed at eliminating any conditions that contribute to a particular species' decline. In extreme cases, some plans can be activated on an emergency basis.

If you make a career in this field, it really helps if you have strong writing skills, for a successful grant application (request for financial support) can make the difference between the success and failure of your project. Almost all nonprofit agencies depend on fund-raising campaigns for support, so some knowledge of marketing and mass-mailing strategies will be valuable. Finally, conservationists must be able to work with media outlets to educate audiences about why animal conservation is in the public interest. Many taxpayers resist the idea of their hard-earned money being invested to protect a class of wild birds, but if it is explained that these birds keep pesky and disease-carrying mosquitoes under control, the expenditure seems more justifiable.

Educational Requirements and Salaries

If you want to direct your own conservation projects, you'll probably need to go all the way to a Ph.D. in one of the life sciences. However, there are many entry-level and middle management–level jobs that are open to those with a bachelor's or master's degree, particularly in the areas of wildlife management, forestry, or ecology. Because this field so often depends on public or charitable contributions, anyone with a keen interest, hours to volunteer, and a knack for raising funds can work his or her way into a species conservation job. Government conservation positions usually start in the low $30,000 range and climb from there. Someone entrusted to manage an entire program or conservation campaign can make a salary above $100,000—but the most common salary is nothing, for virtually all conservation campaigns depend on volunteer work.

15

The Future of Animal Care

If you were to gaze into a crystal ball, what exciting developments would you see unfolding in animal care?

A Space Age Grooming Parlor

Madeline Bright Ogle's fascinating history, "The Heritage of Pet Grooming," offers the following observations on a twenty-first-century pet parlor extraordinaire:

The poor conditions of early pet grooming salons are simply not suitable for the new millennium. The ideal salon of the future has stainless steel tubs with special drain traps designed specifically to catch pet hair. It has an automatic lift to set the larger pets in the bathing tub and a washer and dryer for towels. It includes ceiling-mounted blow-dryers—no more hairballs in the dryer's wheels and enough blowing power on medium heat to dry pets efficiently. The clippers have special wiring that boosts amperage and yet operates at cooler temperatures. It has the latest design in cages, built to last many years. Improved lighting allows employees to check the quality of their work. An emergency generator for power outages allows business activities to continue uninterrupted. The tiled bathing department has maintenance procedures posted.

The advanced sanitation procedures include a "potty-walking" area.

©The Madison Group, Inc.
Posted on: www.petgroomer.com/history/history_2.htm.

While some pets will be more pampered than ever, the use of animal subjects in clinical trials will greatly increase. As a result, there will be more jobs for human caretakers in research settings such as universities and pharmaceutical companies. Protests against the poor treatment of animals have made great headway; expect more monitoring of laboratories in the future and more emphasis on the humane treatment of animal subjects. It will not be surprising to see an entire new category of job arise for specialists who consult on how to get needed data from laboratory animals while minimally invading their bodies or inflicting needless pain and distress.

VETERINARY CARE: CHANGES ON THE HORIZON

There will be big changes in veterinary care, too, as more doctors undertake internships and residencies, and state-of-the-art technology becomes more widely available. This sort of cutting-edge care won't come cheaply, though. For that reason, health insurance for cats, dogs, and exotic pets will become much more commonplace. These policies may not cover recurring problems or routine vaccinations, but they will make all the difference in the case of a catastrophic accident or illness. Health maintenance organizations (HMOs) for pets will also experience a boom, as more veterinarians are already signing up to become preferred providers. In these plans, veterinarians agree to lower their fees for enrolled pets, but they more than make up the loss with additional volume and plan referrals. Veterinary Pet Insurance (VPI) already has 75,000 policyholders in forty-three states and the District of Columbia. Their top-of-the-line policy costs $171 a year for a puppy or kitten and $299 for a ten-year-old, giving a maximum benefit of $4,000 per year. In the next decade, membership in such plans is expected to double or triple as the concept catches on. Other changes to watch for: veterinary Web sites that dispense advice to pet owners over the Internet, veterinary drugs being sold on-line, and more mobile veterinary teams providing service to remote areas at scheduled intervals.

Animal Psychology

There will be a boom in animal psychology. In the last century, the idea of a "pet shrink" was greeted with some amusement, but in the future, animal psychologists will be widely acknowledged for their usefulness in curbing aggressive behavior and assisting with stubborn training problems. Already, several widely syndicated radio programs offer advice from animal psychologists, many of whom specialize in educating owners on whether or not to use reinforcement or aversion training with a troubled pet. They are able to explain "what animals think" so that many problems can be curbed—not by punishing the animal, but by encouraging the human in charge to analyze what factors have contributed to a destructive or annoying habit.

CLONING

Also on the horizon: Cloning technologies involving animals will be used far more widely than they are today. The cloning of laboratory animals, where exact copying is important in establishing an experiment's controls, will become extremely commonplace. Cloning will also be used more often in the production of food animals. Scientists already have developed beef and mutton animals that produce more pounds of meat and resist disease, without being injected with the antibiotics that build resistance in humans.

Companion Animals

It's probable that highly specialized companion animals, such as breeds used for Seeing Eye dogs, will be cloned once there is a greater understanding of which genetic strains encourage a placid temperament coupled with high intelligence. However, experts hotly debate whether animals in sports—like Thoroughbred racing horses—should be cloned. The question is whether cloning a Triple Crown winner, for example, would be good for the sport in terms of producing a championship racer, or bad in terms of taking the element of surprise out of racing results. The debate is an interesting one because although a clone is an "exact copy," no animal *becomes* another. Even if all the genetic material is present to create a champion, variables such as the quality of training or how an animal feels on a given day still may give owners and trainers unlooked-for results.

Cloning and genetically altering animals will make a tremendous difference in the service animal sector, where hundreds of hours and thousands of dollars are invested in teaching dogs to support handicapped owners with simple household tasks. Imagine what a help it will be when a dog designed for longevity and trained to support a paraplegic can stay on the job for fifteen years or longer, instead of just eight, which is the current average. In these cases, trainers will provide initial conditioning, as they do now, and they may establish new "brush up" clinics for older service animals in mid-career. Checks to assure that an animal's cognitive (thinking) functions are still operating at peak capacity will also become part of a mid-career review, at least until scientists, breeders, and trainers gain an understanding of what happens to animals whose lives have been artificially prolonged. They will be working to extend healthy, productive years, not to bioengineer animals to endure an ever lengthening old age.

The Benefits of Cloning

Zoos and animal sanctuaries already expect to reap the benefits of cloning technology. Chinese government experts have predicted the extinction of the beloved giant panda within twelve years, but Beijing scientists recently announced the successful use of cloning technology to create a panda embryo. If further experiments are successful, this could stop the panda's decline.

Genetic Research

In Hawaii, an international team of scientists announced that they cloned three generations of genetically identical mice from adult mouse cells. This technique also may be used to help preserve endangered species. In addition, knowledge gained from the experiment may lead to new ways to research conception, embryo development, aging, cancer, and death in animals and humans.

Recent genetic research has boosted memory and intelligence in mice. Scientists from Princeton University, MIT, and Washington University in St. Louis added an extra modified copy of a natural gene for a protein called nr2b into mouse embryos. Their findings reveal that this extra, perpetually active gene keeps the brain of a mouse primed for new connections all of its life. Scientists hope to someday duplicate the experiment in human subjects.

Other genetic research being conducted by scientists at Purdue University is focused on keeping endangered species healthy when their numbers sharply decline and there is more in-breeding among the fewer remaining animals.

Finally, on the cutting edge of cancer research, several biotech firms in the United States and Europe have spliced human genes onto the DNA of goats, sheep, pigs, and other animals. These genes are designed to produce a specific protein in the animals' milk that will fight human disease. For example, an animal might be bioengineered to produce a protein that would treat hemophilia. Some observers predict that this will result in patients with chronic diseases being able to keep them under control with a regular glass of "designer dairy."

In the years to come, two kinds of jobs will grow within agribusinesses, laboratories, and government agencies. Most obviously, there will be a need for scientists and researchers working on animal subjects. In addition, though, there will be a need for responsible animal managers, people who don't have to have a Ph.D., but who will be very knowledgeable about keeping animal subjects clean, healthy, and problem free.

16

Getting Started in an Animal Care Profession

There are many ways to get experience and to "shadow" animal care professionals so you can see how you truly feel about this kind of work. This is very important for a couple of reasons. First, you'll want to "test your vocation," to see if the animal care field you're considering is really right for you. Second, if you like what you see and decide to go ahead, it will be necessary to prove that you are capable of completing necessary training, including any required certification. Especially if you plan to become a veterinarian or animal preservationist—fields that are highly competitive and require years of postgraduate education—you'll stand a much better chance with any college's or professional school's admissions committee if you can demonstrate that you've had hands-on experience with animals.

Where to Start—4-H Clubs

How do you get such experience? As a start, over six million youth from ages five to nineteen belong to 4-H organizations. Although 4-H has chapters in cities as well as in the country, one of the things it's most famous for is its support of young people who want agribusiness careers. A nonprofit partner of the Department of Agriculture via the National Extension System, one of the things 4-H clubs do is to educate members in breeding and raising livestock. They accomplish this mission through a generous system of grants and scholarships. Many American teenagers receive their first real experiences of raising farm or food animals with the sponsorship of a local 4-H club. If you attend a state fair livestock auction, chances are good that you'll witness bidding on an animal raised by a 4-H member. A 4-H membership is wonderful to cite on college admissions applications because reviewers understand that you've been responsible for animals and you have also been mentored by agribusiness professionals.

Other Options

If 4-H is not available in your community, or if you need to earn a salary while you're gaining experience, identify the animal care facilities in your community. These may be clinics, pet stores, research facilities, kennels, obedience schools, or grooming parlors. Which of them is the most closely related to the professional work you hope to do? Focus on that one business—and as simple as it sounds, pick up the telephone, make an appointment to visit, and prepare your pitch for a part-time job or for volunteer training. If you live in a large community, the classified advertisements can alert you to the facilities that actually need new workers.

Once your foot is in the door, be prepared to present a mini-résumé. This should include your telephone number and address (including an e-mail address if you have one), your school classification (junior, senior), and contact information for two or three references (not family members) who will say positive things about your personal qualities and work habits. Also include brief descriptions of other jobs you've had, even if these are limited to baby-sitting or yard work. The idea is to demonstrate that other people have trusted you to accomplish tasks and that you've followed through reliably.

It really doesn't make any difference to a college or professional school admissions committee whether your early experience is paid or unpaid. Some students have the mistaken impression that volunteer work is somehow loftier than a paid, part-time job. Actually, it makes no difference at all—so if you need some extra cash and are lucky enough to land a paying job, you should not hesitate to take it. Either way, carefully document the experience you've earned when you're ready to ask for admission—whether it be to a veterinary college or to a dog grooming school. Have someone photograph you on the job, so you can include snapshots demonstrating your rapport with four-legged friends.

Grooming, boarding, or cleaning and exercising strays at a city shelter will teach you plenty about whether you'll enjoy spending your working days with other people's pets. If you're interested in large animal care, cattle ranchers and dairy farmers almost always welcome an extra pair of hands. Or you may get a chance to trade mucking labor for horseback rides if you live near a stable, riding school, stud farm, or racetrack. Keep a record of how many hours you work, what tasks you accomplish, and to whom you report. This last item is important because you'll need to ask your supervisor for a letter of reference when the time comes. If you work in a large center with many part-time helpers, it's a plus if you can pull out your logbook to remind your boss of what exactly you've accomplished on the job. Some supervisors even ask student helpers to draft their own letters of recommendation. If this happens to you, include as many details as possible. Don't be afraid to speak up as an advocate for yourself. Who else, after all, is better acquainted with the good job you have done?

How many hours per week do you need to devote to gaining work experience? If you're carrying a heavy academic program, ten is ideal—that's two hours each afternoon Monday through Friday, or two five-hour shifts on Saturday or Sunday. Whatever you do, don't get talked into taking on more work than you can balance comfortably with your family and school responsibilities. Ultimately, it will be your ability to strike a happy, productive balance, and to meet all of your obligations, that will take you the distance.

The important thing is to get work experience before it's time to apply to colleges or professional schools. Now, in fact, is a great time to begin. Establish a positive relationship with your boss, show that you want to take on as much responsibility as possible, and lavish the animals they entrust to you with as much attention as you can possibly give.

Finally, the most obvious work experience is to adopt a pet of your own and establish a long-term caring relationship with it. Don't restrict your duties to feeding and watering—make your pet's environment as stimulating as possible. Schedule time for exercise, play, and grooming, and not only will you perfect your caregiving skills, you'll have made an irreplaceable friend.

Those who care for animals are among the luckiest workers of all. If you decide to join them, whatever your particular job may be, you will enjoy your connection to the animal kingdom as well as your ever growing knowledge and appreciation of the natural world.

All the best wishes for a bright, prosperous, and animal-enriched future!

Glossary

boarder Worker who keeps animals overnight for a set fee, providing food, water, and exercise.

breeder Worker who specializes in husbandry, the scientifically supervised reproduction of animals.

clone Animal reproduced via cellular technology.

companion animal The official term for "pet," an animal domesticated to provide friendship and support to humans.

conservationist College-educated specialist in protecting endangered or rare species.

Cooperative Extension Service Regional government program that may offer training opportunities or support for young adults interested in careers in veterinary medicine.

euthanasia Humanely taking the life of an animal that has been abandoned or is old or too ill to recover its health.

extinction When an animal species dwindles to zero population.

4-H The national, private sector nonprofit partner of the National Extension System, which offers livestock breeding and showing experience to members five to nineteen years of age.

groomer Professionally trained specialist who bathes and trims animals to conform with their breed specifications.

kennel Professional animal boarding facility.

marine biologists Scientists who study all forms of aquatic life.

neuter Surgically sterilize a male or female animal.

parasitology Study of organisms that use other plants and animals as hosts.

preservationist Another term for a specialist in protecting endangered or rare species.

seizure-sensitive dogs Dogs who somehow sense when a human is about to have a seizure; they are trained to alert their owners just before an attack occurs.

service animals Highly trained animals, usually dogs, but occasionally monkeys, who assist blind and mobility-impaired humans with navigation and basic household tasks.

species recovery Planned work done by animal conservation teams to replenish numbers of rare and endangered animals.

trainer Professional who teaches an animal what to do, makes that behavior happen (using humane force if necessary), rewards good results, and punishes mistakes.

veterinarian Doctor for animals; just as doctors for human beings do, veterinarians can specialize after meeting board certification requirements.

veterinary technician Generally a graduate of a two-year community college program, and specially trained to support the work of a veterinarian. The work this staff member does is comparable to how a nurse supports a doctor.

zookeepers These professionals may be zoologists, but they run the gamut from nonprofessional animal caregivers to zoo directors.

zoologist Scientist who studies and classifies members of the animal kingdom, including marine life and tiny animals such as parasites.

Appendix A: Animal Interest and Protection Groups

In the United States

American Animal Hospital Association
P.O. Box 150899
Denver, CO 80215-0899
(303) 986-2800
Web site: http://aahanet.org

American Holistic Veterinary Medical Association
2218 Old Emmorton Road
Bel Air, MD 21015
(410) 569-0795
e-mail: ahvma@compuserve.com

American Veterinarians and Chiropractors Association (AVCA)
623 Main Street
Hillsdale, IL 61257
(309) 658-2920
e-mail: amvetchiro@aol.com

American Zoo and Aquarium Association
8403 Colesville Road, Suite 710
Silver Spring, MD 20910-3314
(301) 562-0777
Web site: http://www.aza.org

Animals and Public Policy
Tufts University
200 Westboro Road
North Grafton, MA 01536
(508) 839-7905
Web site: http://www.tufts.edu/vet/cfa/index.html

Animal Welfare Institute
P.O. Box 3650
Washington, D.C. 20007
(202) 337-2332
Web site: http://www.animalwelfare.com

Friends of Animals
National Headquarters
777 Post Road
Darien, CT 06820
(203) 656-1522
Web site: http://www.friendsofanimals.org

Great Whales Foundation
Box 6847
Malibu, CA 90264
(800) 421-WAVE
Web site: http://elfi.com/gwf

The Guide Dog Foundation for the Blind, Inc.
371 East Jericho Turnpike
Smithtown, NY 11787-2976
(631) 265-2121
Web site: http://www.guidedog.org

International Marine Animal Trainers Association
1200 South Lake Shore Drive
Chicago, IL 60606
Web site: http://www.imata.org

National Animal Interest Alliance
P.O. Box 66579
Portland, OR 97290-6579
(503) 761-1139
Web site: http://www.naiaonline.org

National Association of Animal Breeders
P.O. Box 1033
Columbia, MO 65205
(573) 445-4406
Web site: http://www.naab-css.org/index.html

National Association of Professional Pet Sitters
1030 15th Street NW, Suite 870
Washington, DC 20005
(202) 393-3317
http://www.petsitters.org

New England Anti-Vivisection Society
333 Washington Street, Suite 850
Boston, MA 02108

(617) 523-6020
e-mail: info@ma.neavs.com
Web site: http://www.neavs.org

New Yorkers for Companion Animals
Cat Protection, Dog Protection, No-kill Shelter
1324 Lexington Avenue, Suite 2
New York, NY 10128-1145
(212) 427-8273
e-mail: nyfca@aol.com

Sentient Creatures, Inc.
Cat Protection, Dog Protection, No-kill Shelter
P.O. Box 765, Cathedral Station
New York, NY 10025
(212) 865-5998
e-mail: life1127@aol.com

Wetlands Preserve Environmental and Social Justice Center
161 Hudson Street
New York, NY 10013
(212) 966-4831
Web site: http://www.wetlands-preserve.org

IN CANADA

Animal Alliance of Canada
221 Broadview Avenue, Suite 101
Toronto, ON M4M 2G3
(416) 462-9541

ANIMAL INTEREST AND PROTECTION GROUPS

The Fauna Foundation
P.O. Box 33
Chambly, PQ J3L 4B1
(450) 658-1844

Humane Society of Canada
347 Bay Street, Suite 806
Toronto, ON M5H 2R7
(800) 641-KIND
e-mail: info@humanesociety.com

People for Animal Welfare and Safety (P.A.W.S.)
R.R. 16, Site 14, Box 16
Thunder Bay, ON P7B 6B3
(807) 683-8584

World Wildlife Foundation Canada (WWF)
245 Eglington Avenue East, Suite 410
Toronto, ON M4P 3J1
(800) 26-PANDA

Appendix B: Veterinary Medical Associations

IN THE UNITED STATES

Alabama Veterinary Medical Association
P.O. Box 2370
Auburn, AL 36831-2370
(334) 844-2687
fax: (334) 844-2652
Web site: http://www.alvma.com

Alaska State Veterinary Medical Association
P.O. Box 112269
Anchorage, AK 99511-2269
(907) 279-0454
fax: (907) 279-2335

Arizona Veterinary Medical Association
5502 North 19th Avenue
Phoenix, AZ 85015-7936
(602) 242-7936
fax: (602) 249-3828
e-mail: office@azvma.org
Web site: http://www.azvma.org

VETERINARY MEDICAL ASSOCIATIONS

Arkansas Veterinary Medical Association
8 Shackleford Plaza, Suite 208
Little Rock, AR 72211
(501) 221-1477
fax: (501) 221-6691
e-mail: info@arkvetmed.org
Web site: http://www.arkvetmed.org

California Veterinary Medical Association
5231 Madison Avenue
Sacramento, CA 95841
(916) 344-4985
fax: (916) 344-6147
Web site: http://www.cvma.net

Colorado Veterinary Medical Association
1780 South Bellaire, Suite 210
Denver, CO 80222
(303) 759-1251
fax: (303) 759-1477
e-mail: info@colovma.com
Web site: http://www.colovma.com

Connecticut Veterinary Medical Association
P.O. Box 230
Glastonbury, CT 06033
(800) 659-9683
fax: (860) 657-8244
e-mail: connveterinary@aol.com

Delaware Veterinary Medical Association
937 Monroe Terrace
Dover, DE 19904

(302) 674-8581
Web site: http://www.avma.org/statevma/devma

District of Columbia Veterinary Medical Association
2501 Q Street NW, Suite 320
Washington, DC 20007
(202) 806-6293
fax: (202) 806-4340
Web site: http://www.avma.org/statevma/dcvma

Florida Veterinary Medical Association
7131 Lake Ellenor Drive
Orlando, FL 32809-5738
(407) 851-3862
fax: (407) 240-3710
e-mail: fvma@bellsouth.net
Web site: www.fvma.org

Georgia Veterinary Medical Association
3050 Holcomb Bridge Road
Norcross, GA 30071-1362
(770) 416-1633
fax: (770) 416-9095
e-mail: gvma@mindspring.com

Hawaii Veterinary Medical Association
4400 Kalanianaole Highway, Suite 6
Honolulu, HI 96839-1309
(808) 733-8828

Idaho Veterinary Medical Association
P.O. Box 6573
Boise, ID 83707

(208) 375-1551
fax: (208) 376-4430
e-mail: msvicki@micron.net

Illinois State Veterinary Medical Association
161 South Lincolnway, Suite 302
North Aurora, IL 60542
(630) 892-2321
fax: (630) 892-0818
e-mail: isvma@aol.com
Web site: http://www.avma.org/statevma/ilvma

Indiana Veterinary Medical Association
309 W. Washington Street, Suite 202
Indianapolis, IN 46204
(317) 974-0888
fax: (317) 974-0985
e-mail: ivma@iquest.net
Web site: www.avma.org/statevma/invma

Iowa Veterinary Medical Association
5921 Fleur Drive
Des Moines, IA 50321
(515) 285-6701
fax: (515) 285-7809
e-mail: 74253.1652@compuserve.com

Kansas Veterinary Medical Association
816 SW Tyler, Suite 200
Topeka, KS 66612-1635
(785) 233-4141
fax: (785) 233-2534
Web site: http:// www.vet.ksu.edu/links/kvma

Kentucky Veterinary Medical Association
P.O. Box 4067
Frankfort, KY 40604-4067
(502) 226-KVMA (5862)
fax: (502) 226-6177
e-mail: kvma@aol.com
Web site: www.avma.org/statevma/kyvma

Louisiana Veterinary Medical Association
P.O. Box 14650
Baton Rouge, LA 70808-4650
(800) 524-2996
fax: (225) 926-7242
e-mail: lvma@tlxnet.net
Web Site: http://www.lvma.org

Maine Veterinary Medical Association
P.O. Box 8
Rumford Center, ME 04278
(207) 364-8660
fax: (207) 364-7209
Web site: www.avma.org/statevma/mevma

Maryland Veterinary Medical Association
P.O. Box 439
Fallston, MD 21047-0439
(888) 550-7862
fax: (410) 893-2541
Web site: http://www.mdvma.org

Massachusetts Veterinary Medical Association
169 Lakeside Avenue
Marlborough, MA 01752-4503

VETERINARY MEDICAL ASSOCIATIONS

(508) 460-9333
fax: (508) 460-9969
e-mail: massvet@ma.ultranet.com
Web site: http://www.ultranet.com/~massvet

Michigan Veterinary Medical Association
2144 Commons Parkway
Okemos, MI 48864-3986
(517) 347-4710
fax: (517) 347-4666
e-mail: prescott@michvma.org

Minnesota Veterinary Medical Association
393 North Dunlap Street, Suite 400
St. Paul, MN 55104
(651) 645-7533
fax: (651) 645-7539
e-mail: llacher@mvma.org
Web site: http://www.mvma.org

Mississippi Veterinary Medical Association
209 South Lafayette Street
Starkville, MS 39759
(601) 324-9380
fax: (601) 324-9380

Missouri Veterinary Medical Association
2500 Country Club Drive
Jefferson City, MO 65109
(573) 636-8612
fax: (573) 659-7175
e-mail: movma@socket.net
Web site: http://www.movma.org

Montana Veterinary Medical Association
P.O. Box 6322
Helena, MT 59604
(406) 447-4259
fax: (406) 442-8018
Web site: http://www.avma.org/statevma/mtvma

Nebraska Veterinary Medical Association
P.O. Box 2118
Hastings, NE 68901-2118
(402) 463-4704
fax: (402) 463-5683
Web site: http://www.nvma.org

Nevada Veterinary Medical Association
P.O. Box 34420
Reno, NV 89533
(775) 324-5344
e-mail: nvma@aci.net
Web site: http://www.aci.net/nvma

New Hampshire Veterinary Medical Association
P.O. Box 616
Concord, NH 03302-0616
(603) 224-2432
Fax: (603) 225-0556

New Jersey Veterinary Medical Association
66 Morris Avenue, Suite 2A
Springfield, NJ 07081
(973) 379-1100
e-mail: ralampi@aol.com
Web site: http://www.avma.org/statevma/njvma

VETERINARY MEDICAL ASSOCIATIONS

New Mexico Veterinary Medical Association
3037 San Patricia Place, NW
Albuquerque, NM 87107
(505) 294-1351
e-mail: nmvma@trail.com
Web site: http://www.trail.com/~nmvma

New York City Veterinary Medical Association
331 West 57th Street, S293
New York, NY 10019-3101
(212) 246-0057
e-mail: vmanyc@aol.com

New York State Veterinary Medical Society
9 Highland Avenue
Albany, NY 12205-5417
(518) 437-0787
fax: (518) 437-0957
e-mail: nysvma@albany.net

North Carolina Veterinary Medical Association
138 Spring Avenue
Fuquay-Varina, NC 27526
(919) 557-9385
e-mail: mprasor@cs.com
Web site: http://www.ncvma.org

North Dakota Veterinary Medical Association
921 South 9th St.
Bismarck, ND 58504
(701) 221-7740

Ohio Veterinary Medical Association
3168 Riverside Drive
Columbus, OH 43221
(614) 486-7253
fax: (614) 486-1325
e-mail: ohiovma@ohiovma.org
Web site: http://www.ohiovma.org

Oklahoma Veterinary Medical Association
P.O. Box 14521
Oklahoma City, OK 73113
(405) 478-1002
fax: (405) 478-7163
e-mail: okvma@compuserve.com
Web site: http://www.okvma.org

Oregon Veterinary Medical Association
1880 Lancaster Dr., NE, Suite 118
Salem, OR 97305
(503) 399-0311
fax: (503) 363-4218

Pennsylvania Veterinary Medical Association
P.O. Box 8820
Harrisburg, PA 17105-8820
(717) 558-7750
fax: (717) 558-7845
Web site: http://www.avma.org/statevma/pavma

Rhode Island Veterinary Medical Association
P.O. Box 154
Barrington, RI 02806-0154
(877) 521-0103

e-mail: sslate@rivma.org
Web site: http://www.rivma.org

South Dakota Veterinary Medical Association
South Dakota State University
Dept. of Veterinary Science, Box 2175
Brookings, SD 57007-1396
(605) 688-6649
e-mail: kampmanj@mg.sdstate.edu

Tennessee Veterinary Medical Association
530 Church Street, Suite 700
Nashville, TN 37219
(615) 254-3687
fax: (615) 254-7047
e-mail: tvma@wmgt.org

Texas Veterinary Medical Association
6633 Highway 290 East, Suite 201
Austin, TX 78723
(512) 452-4224
e-mail: texasvma@aol.com
Web site: http://www.tvma.org

Utah Veterinary Medical Association
P.O. Box 6573
Boise, ID 83707
(208) 375-1551
e-mail: msvicki@micron.net

Vermont Veterinary Medical Association
2073 Spear Street
Charlotte, VT 05445

(802) 425-3495
e-mail: smoraska@vbimail.champlain.edu

Virginia Veterinary Medical Association
3108 North Parham Road
Suite 200-B
Richmond, VA 23294
(804) 270-9013
e-mail: vavma@aol.com
Web site: http://www.vvma.org

Washington State Veterinary Medical Association
P.O. Box 962
Bellvue, WA 98009-0962
(425) 454-8381
Web site: http://www.wsvma.org

West Virginia Veterinary Medical Association
201 Virginia Street West
Charleston, WV 25302
(304) 343-6783
Web site: http://www.avma.org/statevma/wvvma

Wisconsin Veterinary Medical Association
301 North Broom Street
Madison, WI 53703
(608) 257-3665
Web site: http://www.wvma.org

Wyoming Veterinary Medical Association
P.O. Box 6573
Boise, ID 83707
(208) 375-1551
e-mail: msvicki@micron.net

Veterinary Medical Associations

In Canada

Canadian Veterinary Medical Association
339 Booth Street
Ottawa, ON KIR 7K1
(613) 236-1162
Web site: http://www.cvma-acmv.org

In Puerto Rico

Puerto Rico Veterinary Medical Association
Colegio de Medicos Veterinarios de Puerto Rico
P.O. Box 360545
San Juan, PR 00936-0545
(787) 283-2840

Alternative, Complementary, and Holistic Veterinary Medicine Associations

Academy of Veterinary Homeopathy (AVH)
751 NE 168th Street
North Miami, FL 33162-2427
(305) 652-5372
e-mail: webmaster@acadvethom.org

The American Academy of Veterinary Acupuncture (AAVA)
P.O. Box 419
Hygiene, CO 80533-0419
(303) 772-6726
e-mail: AAVAoffice@aol.com

American Holistic Veterinary Medical Association (AHVMA)
2218 Old Emmorton Road
Bel Air, MD 21014
(410) 569-0795
e-mail: AHVMA@compuserve.com

American Veterinarians and Chiropractors Association (AVCA)
623 Main Street
Hillsdale, IL 61257
(309) 658-2920
e-mail: AmVetChiro@aol.com

Florida Holistic Veterinary Medical Association
751 Northeast 168th Street
North Miami Beach, FL 33162-2427
(305) 652-5372

Georgia Holistic Veterinary Medical Association
334 Knollwood Lane
Woodstock, GA 30188
(770) 516-5954

Greater Washington DC Area Holistic Veterinary Association
6136 Brandon Avenue
Springfield, VA 22150
(703) 503-8690

Veterinary Medical Associations

Great Lakes Holistic Veterinary Medical Association
9824 Durand Avenue
Sturtevant, WI 53177
(414) 886-1100

International Veterinary Acupuncture Society (IVAS)
P.O. Box 1478
Longmont, CO 80502
(303) 682-1167
e-mail: IVASOffice@aol.com

Rocky Mountain Holistic Veterinary Medical Association
311 South Pennsylvania Street
Denver, CO 80209
(303) 733-2728

Appendix C: Recommended Web Sites and Journals

WEB SITES

Absaroka Search Dogs
http://www.wtp.net/asdk9sar

Alternative Veterinary Medicine
http://www.altvetmed.com

American Dog Trainers Network (State by State Directory)
http://www.inch.com/%7Edogs/service.html

American Rescue Dog Association
http://www.ardainc.org/

American Veterinary Medical Association: Veterinary Technician Programs
http://www.avma.org/care4pets/vtprog.htm

Animal Wellness International
http://www.animalwellnessintl.com

Canine Companions for Independence
http://www.caninecompanions.org

Recommended Web Sites and Journals

College of Veterinary Medicine/Michigan State University
http://cvm.msu.edu

Cornell Veterinary Medical Teaching Hospital
http://www.vet.cornell.edu/hospital/edu.htm

Exotic Animals: Care and Conservation Resource Site
http://www.pacificnet.net/~jmcnary/

Hearing Dogs
http://deafness.about.com/health/deafness/msubhdog.htm

Horse Training from the Ground Up
http://horsetraining.8k.com

Marine Biology Web Page
http://life.bio.sunysb.edu/marinebio/mbweb.html

PAWS Wildlife Center
http://www.paws.org/wildlife

PetGroomer.com
http://www.petgroomer.com

Preparation for a Career in Marine Biology
http://www-marine.stanford.edu/hmsweb/webster.html

The Seeing Eye
http://www.seeingeye.org/

Service Dog Directory
http://wolfpacks.com/serviced.htm

Training Your Dog by Cindy Tittle Moore
http://www.k9web.com/dog-faqs/training.html

U.S. Fish and Wildlife Service
http://endangered.fws.gov

Veterinary Internet Resource Network (UK)
http://www.vetscape.co.uk

The Veterinary Technician
http://www.avma.org/care4pets/caretech.htm

Vet On-Line
http://www.priory.com/vet.htm

Working Dogs Cyberzine
http://www.workingdogs.com

World Wide Web Virtual Library: Veterinary Medicine
http://netvet.wustl.edu/vetmed.htm

JOURNALS

Bellwether, The Newsmagazine of the School of
Veterinary Medicine, University of Pennsylvania
http://www.vet.upenn.edu/comm/publications/bellwether/bellw.html

The Canadian Veterinary Journal
339 Booth Street
Ottawa, ON K1R 7K1
(613) 236-1162 ext. 17

RECOMMENDED WEB SITES AND JOURNALS

Journal of Veterinary Dentistry
Veterinary Hospital of the University of Pennsylvania
3900 Delancy Street, #3113
Philadelphia, PA 19104
(215) 573-8135
fax: (215) 898-9937
e-mail: cschust@vet.upenn.edu

Journal of Veterinary Medical Education
VA-MD College of Veterinary Medicine
Virginia Polytechnic Institute and State University
Blacksburg, VA 24061

Journal of Wildlife Diseases
Wildlife Disease Association
P.O. Box 1897
Lawrence, KS 66044-8897

Journal of Zoo and Wildlife Medicine
American Association of Zoo Veterinarians
P.O. Box 1897
Lawrence, KS 66044-8897
(785) 843-1235
fax: (785) 843-1274
e-mail: orders@allenpress.com

Veterinary Technician Journal
Veterinary Learning Systems
425 Phillips Boulevard #100
Trenton, NJ 08618
e-mail: 1cranke@cvma-acmv.org

For Further Reading

Ainslie, Tom, and Bonnie Ledbetter. *The Body Language of Horses: Revealing the Nature of Equine Needs, Wishes, and Emotions and How Horses Communicate Them—For Owners, Breeders, and Trainers.* New York: William Morrow & Company, 1980.

Bailey, Gwen. *Adopt the Perfect Dog: A Practical Guide to Choosing and Training an Adult Dog.* Pleasantville, NY: Readers Digest, 2000.

Carlson, Delbert G. *Cat Owner's Home Veterinary Handbook.* Foster City, CA: IDG Books Worldwide, 1995.

Checchi, Mary Jane. *Are You the Pet for Me? Choosing the Right Pet for Your Family.* New York: St. Martin's Press, 1999.

Cooper, Paulette. *277 Secrets Your Snake Wants You to Know: Unusual and Useful Information for Snake Owners and Snake Lovers.* Berkeley, CA: Ten Speed Press, 1999.

Coren, Stanley. *How to Speak Dog: Mastering the Art of Dog-Human Communication.* New York: Free Press, 2000.

For Further Reading

———. *The Intelligence of Dogs: A Guide to the Thoughts, Emotions, and Inner Lives of Our Canine Companions.* New York: Bantam Books, 1995.

Crisp, Terri. *Out of Harm's Way: The Extraordinary True Story of One Woman's Lifelong Devotion to Animal Rescue.* New York: Pocket Books, 1997.

Freeman, Derek. *Barking Up the Right Tree: Breeding, Rearing and Training the Guide Dog Way.* Lydney, Gloucestershire, U.K.: Ringpress Books Ltd, 1993.

Giffin, James M., et al. *Horse Owner's Veterinary Handbook.* Foster City, CA: IDG Books Worldwide, 1998.

Herriot, James. *Animal Stories.* New York: St. Martin's Press, 1997.

Herriot, James. *Every Living Thing.* New York: St. Martin's Press, 1996.

Hess, Elizabeth. *Lost and Found: Dogs, Cats, and Everyday Heroes at a Country Animal Shelter.* New York: Harcourt Brace, 1998.

Hill, Cherry. *Horse and Rider.* Pownal, VT: Storey Books, 1995.

Lyons, John. *Lyons on Horses: John Lyons' Proven Conditioned-Response Training Program.* New York: Doubleday, 1991.

New Skete Monks. *The Art of Raising a Puppy.* Boston: Little, Brown and Company, 1991.

Stotsky, Sandra, and Jan Mahood. *Adopting a Dog (Cats and Dogs: A Basic Training, Caring, and Understanding Library)*. New York: Chelsea House Publishing, 1998.

Vogel, Colin. *Complete Horse Care Manual.* New York: DK Publishing, 1995.

Index

A
acupuncture, 25, 26
agribusiness, 2, 26–27, 86, 87–88
American Association of Zoo Keepers, 67
American Dog Trainers' Network, 38
American Fisheries Society, 71
American Holistic Veterinary Society, 24, 26
American Rescue Dog Association, 46
American Society for the Prevention of Cruelty to Animals (ASPCA), 11, 38
American Veterinary Medical Association (AVMA), 1, 12, 18, 25

animal
  adoption worker, 73–77
  breeding/husbandry, 4–6, 24, 27, 51–54, 63, 87
  conservationists/preservationists, 7, 78–80, 87
  control workers, 7–8
  groomers, 1, 6, 7, 10, 55, 456, 58–61, 74, 81–82, 88, 89
  hospitals/clinics, 13, 28, 29, 55, 56, 58, 88
  psychologists, 83
  shelters, 15, 73–75, 89
  trainers 1, 3, 34–50, 63
Animal Behavior Center, 38
animal care, history of, 9–12

animal rights
  activists/protests, 47–48, 74, 82
animals
  abandoned, 8, 73, 74
  boarding them, 6, 55–57, 89
  exotic, 2, 4, 22, 23, 24, 29, 67, 82
  food/meat, 12, 26–27, 29, 52, 84, 88
  in movies and television, 4, 6, 35
  performance/circus, 4, 35, 37, 47–48
  service, 3, 4, 10, 84–85
  and therapy, 44–45
  wild/wildlife, 2, 3, 4, 18, 22, 48, 68, 78–80
  work, 11, 34
animals as companions/pets, 1, 4, 6, 9, 11, 12, 18, 24, 29, 53, 55–57, 73–75, 84, 90
Association of Women Veterinarians, 12

B
Bergh, Peter, 11

C
Canine Companions for Independence, 43

cats, 1, 4, 5, 13, 14, 15, 18, 25, 34, 44, 52, 54, 56, 62, 64, 73–74, 76, 82–83
cattle/livestock, 4, 5, 9, 10, 13, 24, 27, 51, 52, 87–88, 89
certification, 19–21, 38, 51, 58, 61, 87
cloning, 5, 27, 52–53, 83–84
college courses/BA degree, 2, 7, 16–17, 27, 29, 51, 65, 68, 70, 71, 80, 87, 88, 89, 90
Cooperative Extension Service, 15

D
Department of Fish and Wildlife, 22
dogs, 1, 4, 5, 9–10, 13, 14, 15, 18, 44, 48–49, 52, 53–54, 56, 59, 60, 62, 64, 73–74, 76, 82–83
  antiterrorist/bomb sniffer, 3–4, 46
  disabled/handicapped people and, 44, 84–85
  hearing/Hearing Ear, 3, 43

search and rescue, 3, 4, 15, 45–46
Seeing Eye, 3, 10, 34, 41–42, 84
seizure-sensitive, 3, 43–44
dog trainers, 38–47
dog-walking, 15

E
endangered species, 7, 66, 78–79, 86
Endangered Species Act of 1973, 79
euthanasia, 8, 23, 73, 74

F
fish, 1, 9, 27, 51, 63, 71
food safety, 29
4-H clubs, 87–88

G
genetic research, 85–86

H
high school, 15–16
holistic medicine, 24–26
homeopathy, 25
horses, 1, 2, 6, 10, 13, 24, 25, 34, 51, 52, 56, 89
horse/equine trainers, 35–37, 51, 84
humane/protection societies, 3, 11, 73

I
Internet, 7, 28, 62, 65, 76, 83
internships, 2, 19–20, 23, 27, 82

L
lab animals, 52, 82, 83
Leininger, Dr. Mary Beth, 12
letter of recommendation, 89–90

M
marine biologists, 7, 70–72
mentoring programs, 15
military, 3, 12, 15, 29, 37, 45, 46–47

N
National Association of Dog Obedience Instructors, 38
National Association of Professional Pet Sitters, 57
National Extension System, 87
National Wildlife Federation, 22
New Skete shepherds, 53

O
obedience training 7, 38–40, 42–43, 48, 49–50, 88

P

parasitology, 68
part-time work, 14, 28, 88–90
People for the Ethical Treatment of Animals (PETA), 47
pet-sitters, 56–57
pet store owners, independent, 6–7, 62–64
pet superstores, 6–7, 58, 62, 64–65
Ph.D.s/research doctors, 4, 7, 23, 68, 69, 70, 71, 72, 80, 86
professors, 67, 68–69, 70, 71
puppy raisers, 41

R

residencies, 2, 19, 21, 27, 82
résumés, 88–89
Royal Society for the Prevention of Cruelty to Animals (RSPCA), 11

S

Scripps Institution of Oceanography, 72

T

tigers, 34, 48, 49–50
training programs, 15, 31, 38–39, 46, 51, 58–59, 61, 87–88, 90

U

U.S. Fish and Wildlife Service, 79

V

veterinarians (DVMs), 1, 2, 3, 4, 6, 7, 11–12, 13–21, 22–28, 30, 32, 38, 54, 57, 63, 74, 82–83, 87
veterinary medicine, college of, 2, 10–11, 12, 13, 14, 16–20, 27, 28, 89
veterinary specialties, 2, 18, 20, 22, 23–27
veterinary technicians/technologists, 1, 3, 4, 6, 7, 29–33, 65, 74
volunteering, 7, 14, 46, 67, 73, 74–77, 80, 88, 89

W

women as vets, 12, 28

Z

zoologists, 7, 66–69
zoos, 3, 22, 29, 66–67, 68

www.ingramcontent.com/pod-product-compliance
Lightning Source LLC
Chambersburg PA
CBHW052056070526
44584CB00017B/2204